Stand and Deliver

Communicators. The most important management skill is communication. The authors of this series are all specialists in the art.

Blank Page To First Draft In 15 Minutes
The most effective shortcut to preparing a speech or presentation.
Phillip Khan-Panni

2-4-6-8 How Do You Communicate?
How to make your point in just a minute
Phillip Khan-Panni

"Phillip Khan-Panni is regarded as the foremost authority in Britain on precise and concise communication."

Resolving Conflict
Establish trusting and productive relationships in the workplace
Shay & Margaret McConnon

Communicators is an imprint of How To Books.
For further details please send for a free copy of the latest catalogue
3 Newtec Place, Magdalen Road, Oxford OX4 1RE United Kingdom

Stand and Deliver

Leave them stirred,
not shaken

Phillip Khan-Panni

communicators

Published by How To Books Ltd,
3 Newtec Place, Magdalen Road,
Oxford OX4 1RE, United Kingdom.
Tel: (01865) 793806. Fax: (01865) 248780
email: info@howtobooks.co.uk
http://www.howtobooks.co.uk

First edition 2002

British Library Cataloguing in Publication Data.
A catalogue record for this book is available from the British Library.

Edited by Nikki Read
Cover design by Baseline Arts Ltd, Oxford

Produced for How To Books by Deer Park Productions
Typeset by PDQ Typesetting, Newcastle-under-Lyme, Staffordshire
Printed and bound in Great Britain

NOTE: The material contained in this book is set out in good faith for general
guidance and no liability can be accepted for loss or expense incurred as a
result of relying in particular circumstances on statements made in this book.
Laws and regulations are complex and liable to change, and readers should
check the current position with the relevant authorities before making
personal arrangements.

Communicators is an imprint of How To Books.

Contents

and the United States, one of the most popular sessions is called
'Meet the Pros', a chance to get up close and conversational with
experts in different aspects of the speaking business. Find out how to
place a value on your ideas.

5 Developing your Topic   54

'What shall I talk about?' That is one of the main concerns of a
budding professional speaker, and the one that distinguishes
professionals from amateurs. This chapter guides you along the path
to becoming the kind of expert that people will pay to hear, and
explains the difference between the two main kinds of experts that
become public speakers.

6 Structuring your Speech   67

Making a speech is much more than hurling a script at an
audience. It must take account of their needs, and make it easy for
them to follow and agree. This is about focus as much as about
structure, and it will benefit a speaker as much as it will benefit
the audience. It offers a simple sequence that will help any speech to
connect a speaker with the audience.

7 The Language you Use   79

Do you write your speeches to be read or to be heard? The language
we use for the ear should be very different from the language for the
eye. This chapter considers the right kind of vocabulary, rhythm,
and how to meet your listeners halfway. It encourages you to use
memorable phrases and sound bites, as well as energy and
oratorical devices to push the buttons in the hearts of your hearers.

8 Improving the Way you Sound   92

As a speaker, you use your voice. But do you like the way you
sound? Can you change it? This chapter covers such essentials as
breathing correctly, projecting your voice, and developing vocal
variety to sound much more interesting. Plus those reliable
standards, Pitch, Pace and Pauses. There are even a couple of
exercises that you can do in the car or in the bath to add resonance
to your voice. Worth it for any speaker.

9 Sounds and Pictures

Have you ever heard of the 'Mozart effect'? There is scientific evidence that certain sounds, including the music of Mozart, can improve brain function. By choosing words that work, a speaker can dramatically improve the audience's receptiveness. This chapter also deals with the use of mental images, not only to help listeners' understanding, but also to improve the speaker's memory.

10 Connecting with the Audience

Ever thought a speaker is someone with the gift of the gab? Prepare to lose that notion. This chapter is about having something to say that's worth hearing ... and about understanding the make-up of any audience. It considers six typical types of listener, as well as four levels of communication, and gives some sound advice (no pun intended!) on microphone technique.

11 Deliver with Confidence

How do you take charge of the stage, and when should you switch on your 'platform presence'? To paraphrase a popular song, it ain't what you say but the way that you say it ... This chapter will open your eyes to the way you are perceived by an audience, from the moment they set eyes on you. Here you will find tips on taking charge, handling 'Listener's Drift', and the importance of letting them see your eyes.

12 Gestures and Movement

Do your gestures help or hinder your communication? Find out what works and why. This chapter will alert you to the gestures that irritate or alienate an audience, and guide you in making the kind of moves that make you look good and feel good. When your posture is right, your attitude improves, and you even sound better!

About the author

Dedication

To Fr Van, still at 'the school on the hill', who started me on the road to public speaking, and whom I still love dearly.

To Fr Joseph Killoran, who always believed in me as a writer and became my friend.

To Evelyn, who supported me in so many ways, and especially in the run-up to the heart bypass that imposed the deadline for completing this book.

To Debbie, my business partner, who took me by the shoulders and turned me to face in the direction she knew I should be travelling.

My grateful thanks to them all. They may never know how much they have helped.

Preface

I was 12 years old when I made my first speech. It was such an embarrassing experience that I can still recall the way my glasses fogged up and my shirt clung to my back, as wet as my hair and forehead. There was a ringing inside my head and I was in a state of almost terminal tension.

Fr Gerard Van Walleghem (Fr Van to his friends) was the man responsible. He was my class teacher, and he introduced many new ideas. Speechmaking was one of them. I'd never knowingly heard a speech before, beyond the regular perorations by the Headmaster of my boarding school. However, Fr Van decided that, because I talked a lot (Quiet! You at the back of the class ...!) I should go first.

Unfortunately, neither did I understand what was expected of me, nor was I able to ask for help. If I was to be the role model, I told myself, then Father Van must have had expectations of me, and I must therefore live up to those expectations without revealing my ignorance.

'We are going to start speech-making,' said Father Van. 'You can go first.'

'Thanks, Father.' Proud to be first, but terrified too.

'You know what to do?'

'Er ...'

'Think of a subject, write down what to say about it, then memorize it.'

'What should I talk about?'

'You choose. It can be about anything at all.'

I agonized for a couple of days to no effect, and eventually chose as my subject an incident from the previous winter vacation, covering three foolscap pages with untidy handwriting. In those days, as now, I had good writing on some days, and a poor scrawl on others. This was one of the latter. What I wrote amounted to no more than an essay, and not a very interesting one. It was odd that even though I had often been complimented as a wordsmith, with a wide vocabulary, faultless grammar, and a knack for narrative, when I came to write my text for this speech I was pedestrian and without focus. Perhaps it was because, when I wrote essays and articles for the school magazine, I could let myself go, knowing that I would not be present when they were read. However, I would be very much present when the text of my speech was revealed, so I became tense and inhibited, abandoning my natural sense of written humour and seeking shelter in the linear account of the event I had chosen.

The narrative concerned a foolhardy episode in which two friends and I spied on a female guest sunbathing naked on the flat roof of the Grand Hotel in Calcutta.

She was white and foreign, possibly English or American, and the prospect of seeing a naked white woman was, in those post-Colonial days, even more exciting. In order to see without being seen, it was necessary to take a foolhardy risk, high above the ground, under attack from marauding hawks that wanted us for lunch. My friends gave up, and were roundly scolded by the naked lady, but I remained concealed, gaining the best view and the plaudits of my friends, along with scratches on my back and arms from the swooping hawks.

However, why I supposed anyone would be interested in such a silly episode I cannot now imagine. At any rate, it was a poor speech, lacking focus or purpose, but which I delivered with gusto from the stage in a voice that had full volume but no vocal variety. Halfway through this inept declamation, Father Van stopped me. He paused while he rehearsed what he was going to say, searching for a kindly turn of phrase.

Gently he asked about the point of the story and his questions were clearly designed to help me achieve some sort of focus. I answered him mechanically, terrified of losing the tension that was holding me together. When he signalled for me to start again, not from the beginning but from a recent paragraph, I shook with fear of forgetting my lines. But somehow my mind went into cruise control and the words came tumbling out again, almost exactly the same as the first time. Like a middle distance runner ending with a sprint, I lunged at the finishing line and stood panting on the stage, not knowing if I'd be required to endure the agony all over again, and waiting for permission to descend.

The requisite words of release were spoken and I became unfrozen, stumbling down the steps at one side of the proscenium arch. I sat in isolation in the body of the hall as the next boy went up to deliver his speech, but I neither heard any of it nor recall who he was. Instead, I unravelled my three foolscap pages of text, noticed the instructions I had written to myself at the top right hand corner, and went over the entire speech in my mind, re-living every dreadful moment, and telling myself where and how I could have been so much better.

In more recent times, I have achieved some success in public speaking, and have tried to pass on some of what I have learned in this book. My hope is that you will never suffer as I did, aged twelve, nor ever deliver a boring speech. Two days after writing this, I shall be having a heart bypass operation, so my message to you is this: whenever you rise to make a speech, make it your intention to take your listeners by the heart.

Leave them stirred, not shaken.

Phillip Khan-Panni

Chapter 1

You don't have to be a born speaker

In this Chapter:

◆ **are good speakers born or made?**

◆ **what made one speaker surprisingly good**

◆ **putting the right filters in place**

◆ **speak to one listener at a time.**

In her Churchill Lecture in 1991, Her Royal Highness The Princess Royal said:

> It is possible to communicate successfully with or without language, as long as we understand the fundamental desires of human nature. Having a firm grasp of the English language, with its abundant vocabulary, permits us to explain anything in a myriad of different ways, so long as we remain aware of our own limitations in employing it.

I have always admired orators. They are men and women who can make me laugh or cry, rouse me to anger or passion, bring about some change in me. With words. I have always wanted to be one of them, and as I advanced my public speaking career, I developed a style that was passionate rather than measured, more emotional than reasoned. It became my idea of the best oratorical style. I therefore tended to prefer speakers with an evangelical style, those who can reach into your very being and shake you warmly by the heart. I have always admired those who are fluent in the vocabulary of ideas as well as of words, eloquent with emotion, and possessed of a rich bass-baritone voice, if male, or a mellow contralto if female. That was my starting position.

I started to retreat from that position when people started asking me, **'Are good speakers born or made?'** I'm never sure why they ask that question.

◆ Is it just the standard conversational gambit when talking to a professional speaker, or

◆ do they mean to ask whether they have any chance of becoming a good speaker?

◆ Are they asking if it takes talent alone, or

◆ will hard work get them there?

Although I wasn't sure why they were asking, I did start to think about the right answer, and I have come to believe that you don't have to be a born speaker to be a good one. This was well illustrated for me by a recent training assignment. Let me tell you about it.

A number of financial institutions were due to make a combined representation to a government department in London, and one director from each company was appointed to make a presentation on a part of the whole case. I was brought in to coach them individually. Each director was very different from all the others. **Director A** turned up with his 'minder' – a creative person whose role was to prepare the words and pictures for his boss's presentations. Director A was clever, articulate and quick-witted, but I could see that his self-confidence was brittle, and he felt he needed a formula to follow.

His performance on the day turned out to be nervous and unsure, although he had improved the organization of his material. He was fine once he got into his stride, but he gave the impression of trying for effect. He wasn't really speaking from the heart.

Director B looked younger than he was, and he was anxious to learn. An accountant by training, he was not a natural presenter, and his prepared material was far from good enough. We totally reconstructed his story, and developed a powerful 'hook' that would launch him into his message. Over a two-day period we had three brief sessions together and **he improved out of all recognition**, because he started to **speak with conviction**, whereas he had started out thinking he had only to read or recite his script. His performance was one of the better ones, marked by sincerity, conviction and a desire to persuade his listeners.

Director C came into the picture late, because of 'diary commitments', or so I was told. I came to believe that he had little faith in training. Although he'd never had training before, he was a powerful presenter, and he knew his stuff, so why would he need help from me?

That said, he was sufficiently curious to turn up and sample what I had to offer. We first met at the buffet lunch during the dress rehearsal, and he asked me a couple of questions about presentation technique. He liked my answers and asked to have a brief session with me later. When it was over, he said, **'That was excellent training. You didn't give me lots of formulas. Instead you took my complex subject, simplified it, and in a few minutes showed me a much better way to put it across.'** He not only did well, but he felt good about his performance.

Director D was a lady with an academic background. As a PhD, she was deeply knowledgeable about her subject, and her brief was to provide the economic justification for the case that the team was putting forward. She knew how to present because she had been a lecturer for several years. However, no one had ever talked to her about the difference between lecturing and persuading (which was the object of the exercise before us). As soon as she had grasped that difference, she was off like a rocket, and her performance was polished and believable, although not passionate. Her style matched her profile.

Director E was the revelation. Like Director A, he arrived with his own wordsmith and the material for a PowerPoint presentation that he had not yet put together. While he was running through his stuff, I was struck by two things: one, he was proposing to act as chairman only, introducing each member of his team while making no significant contribution to their case; and two, he was easily the team's best presenter.

This surprised me because **his speaking style was avuncular**, not passionate at all. And yet, he had the ability to captivate his listeners and leave them stirred, not shaken! Something about his voice made him easy on the ear, and he had an attractive hint of a Celtic accent. It was that *he enjoyed communicating*. When he spoke you could tell that he had things to say and he wanted you to hear them, he wanted you to know what he knew, he wanted you to feel as he did about his subject. There was the start of a smile in his voice, a warmth that you could sense without being able to pinpoint it, and an easy fluency that you could admire as you prepared to listen all day.

I think he was surprised when I told him, 'You are outstandingly the best presenter in the pack. You must take a greater share of the message.' It surprised him because he was prepared to be chairman, introducing and linking the other speakers, facilitating rather than leading. But he had what it takes to be a great speaker, even though he was not cast in the mould of the orators I have always admired. I helped him to identify what gave him his edge, and how he could apply it consistently.

Having realized what it was, the question in my mind was, **could I bottle it**? Could I take what gave him that edge, make it general, and teach it to others? The answer is ... yes. Director E had the advantage of starting with natural talent, but talent alone is not enough. You have to do something with it. And that 'something' can be taught to others who may not have the talent, but who do have the desire to be good speakers.

Hence this book. The core message of this book is that *if you put the right filter in place, you will connect with your listeners*, and they will want to hear what you have to say. You will then have the opportunity to touch their hearts and make a difference to them. You will be able to give them a new outlook, a different perspective, a fresh approach to their lives or to the subject of your talk.

Of course you will need techniques, and you will find them here. In this book you will find ways of putting your speeches together, and guidance in putting them across. I shall cover the techniques of:

◆ platform presence

◆ gestures and movement

◆ vocal variety

◆ developing your voice.

I shall cover every important part of speechmaking, from preparation through to the introduction, and on to the standing ovation. But the central message is this: **have something to say and really want to say it**, not for your own sake, but for the sake of your listener.

Note that I said 'listener' – singular, not plural. You may have 30 listeners, or 300 or 3,000. But don't speak to 30 or 300 or 3,000. **Speak to one at a time.** Speak as though there were only one listener, and as if you had developed your message just for that one listener. It will make an amazing difference to your level of sincerity.

This book will offer you some techniques for putting your speech together and a bit more on putting it across, but that is not its main purpose. It aims, instead, to open your understanding of what happens when you stand before an audience with a bag of ideas in your hand or in your head, and come face to face with the test of your own sincerity. My purpose is to help you to speak with impact, and to **leave your audience stirred, not shaken**.

Whenever I coach someone in public speaking or making a presentation, I notice how different they sound when they are trying to remember their script, compared with when they are telling me what they know and believe. One client was typical: he was giving a talk to 50 middle and senior managers about their management style. The conversation went a bit like this:

What's your theme? Management styles.

Who will be there? About 50 managers and directors from around Britain.

Why will they be there? Because they have been told to come.

What are you going to tell them? That they should be leaders.

(So far I was getting nowhere, and he was screwing up

his face as he tried to remember his prepared presentation. Fast forward a little.)

How many management styles will you cover, seven?
No, six.

What are they? (He listed them.)

Which is the right style? (He came alive.) There isn't one. No single management style is the right one at all times. Good managers are flexible. Sometimes they need to say, 'Do this because I say so.' At other times they need to be democratic, or empathic, or persuasive. They need to be sensitive to the circumstance and adapt their approach accordingly.

So what's your message? I want to urge them to be better managers. No, I want to inspire them to be *leaders.* I want to tell them that leadership gets results and the right leadership gets *extraordinary* results.

So what changed? Once I asked him about 'management' he found himself on familiar territory. Not only that, he had a bee in his bonnet about flexible, variable management styles. He had things to say about how managers should run their departments, and he wanted to say them. *The message came from within him.* It was his passion. He understood that his skill on the platform would grow when he spoke from the heart, not from being drilled in platform or vocal techniques.

When he found his message, he found his voice.

In summary . . .

- ◆ Princess Anne once said to beware of the limitations of language.
- ◆ I no longer believe that good speakers are born.
- ◆ Different speaking styles can be compelling – even the avuncular style.
- ◆ What matters is the right attitude and the appropriate filter.
- ◆ Speak to a single individual if you want to identify your message.
- ◆ Identify your message and you'll find your speaking voice.

Chapter 2

Deliver a speech worth hearing

In this Chapter:

◆ **how do you sound to others?**

◆ **are you true to yourself when you speak?**

◆ **do you care about your listeners' needs?**

◆ **have something to say**

◆ **really want to say it**

◆ **develop the right skills .. and attitude of mind**

◆ **make every speech a performance.**

He was the managing director of a retailing establishment. He was well known in his trade, because his was a family business, and three generations of his family before him had served on various trade committees, and he himself was a past president of his trade association. Over the years he had made many a speech, within the trade, at the golf club, and in the other groups that he had joined as part of his social circle. He claimed that making a speech was as easy as falling off a log.

His trade association's secretary called me on the telephone. 'The man's a disaster,' he confided. 'He is down to deliver the keynote address at our next annual conference, and I'm afraid he will bore the delegates out of their skulls and totally ruin the conference. Can you help?'

The two views of the same man's public speaking skills could not have been further apart. 'What's wrong with his speechmaking?' I asked. There was a long groan, then:

> He simply reads his script from the lectern. His delivery is monotonous and indistinct. He puts on his reading glasses, buries his head in the text, mumbles his way from start to finish without looking up at the audience, then departs with a self-satisfied smirk, as though he has just delivered the word of the Delphic Oracle.

Does that sound like anyone you know? I said it was not unusual, and that many – too many – people in business believe that their audiences are dying to hear any pronouncement they care to make, so they don't deem it necessary to consider the needs of their listeners. I then added that I could not help unless the man agreed that he needed help, and quoted a piece of doggerel that I had written some years before, when giving a talk to a toastmasters club about making a speech that people would want to hear. It went like this:

> Like waves that crash on seaside sands,
> The audience claps its fevered hands;
> Prolonged applause, and maybe cheers,
> Will fill your eyes with grateful tears.
> But that can only be your due
> If to yourself your speech is true.

The relevance to the assembled toastmasters was that many of them also made speeches that satisfied their own purposes, and paid little or no attention to the needs of the audience. They are not really speeches, but rather scripts thrown at the audience.

The first requirement of a speech is a **message**. That means much more than information. It implies a point of view, it implies a purpose to the communication, it implies some value in what is being said, both to the speaker and to the audience. As I never tire of saying, if all you want to do is communicate information, send an e-mail, or put it on one side of a small piece of paper and send it to your audience. Then the recipients can read and absorb it when it is most convenient, and can do so faster than you can tell it. So, transmitting information can be done more efficiently in writing. When you make a speech you must have a larger purpose: **you must have something to say**.

The next requirement is to **really want to say it**. It should be something you believe in deeply, not only for yourself, but also for others:

♦ you want to tell them about it

♦ persuade them of its significance

♦ encourage them to make it part of their own values or attitudes.

Even if you got the idea from someone else originally, the message must belong to you, in that you have made it part of your thinking and put your own spin on it. Don't merely regurgitate what you have heard from someone else. I once heard a speaker who was a poor man's **Tony Robbins**. He was so impressed by the American that he copied him, right down to the details of wearing a headphone, dressing casually in black sweatshirt and jeans, and repeatedly smacking the back of one hand into the palm of the other (Robbins smacks his chest). I kept thinking, 'Why do I need to listen to this second-hand stuff? If I want to hear Tony Robbins' material (and attitudes), I can get a video of the original.'

Your speech must be *your* point of view, something you believe in, and which can be identified with you. That's why I call this ingredient the Messenger. It's about you. However, you must want your listeners to do something with it. A speech that does not bring about some change in the thinking, attitude or behaviour of your listeners is no more than an entertainment. That's fine if you wish to limit your speaking career to the after dinner circuit, but it's not good enough for a business or motivational or inspirational speaker.

Even if you are not a professional speaker, even if you are just improving your skills at Toastmasters International or some other speakers' club, and especially if you are hoping to succeed in speech competitions, you need to understand the importance of speaking from heart to heart. Audiences can tell if you are sincere or not. In two speech contests that I entered, both at advanced levels, I came second because of my state of mind.

On one of those occasions I had had several angry phone calls on my mobile phone, from someone close to me, just before the contest. Then in the ballot for speaking order, I drew no. 1, believing that the first speaker almost never wins, and finally, the contest chairman not only did not warm up the audience, but he left the lectern in the middle of the speaking area, so that I had to carry it to one side before starting my speech. He wanted to shake my hand but I would have preferred to shake him warmly by the throat. When I turned to face the audience, I was seething inwardly, and when I smiled at them they knew it wasn't a genuine, happy smile, but more like the baring of teeth before an attack! No wonder the judges placed me second.

The third vital ingredient is **method**. Once again, if the content alone matters, then why not send it in writing and save everyone's time? A speaker who does not take the trouble to develop technique is at risk of being boring, and no one has the right to be boring. Such a speaker may also be seen as arrogant. There are certain skills that enhance delivery, and certain techniques that are generally expected of a speaker.

One good way to discover whether you need to work on this ingredient is to make a speech in front of a video camera, then play it back to a couple of close friends (who are not afraid to tell you the truth) and ask them – and yourself – this simple question: 'Would you pay to hear that person speak?' Seriously, would you pay to hear you speak? How much would you pay?

Now ask your friends these other questions, and have them write down their answers:

1. **What was the core message?**

2. **What was the sequence of the argument?**

3. **Did you agree with/accept what was said?**

4. **What will you do differently in future as a result of that speech?**

5. **What did you do well?**

6. **What would they like you to do differently?**

Can you see how this process will help you to achieve a sharper focus? It will help you to assess whether the speech works, and what you need to work on to make it succeed even more effectively. If time allows, you should always apply this test to any major speech you plan to give. People want to hear your expertise, but they will not readily endure a poor performance, especially if they have paid to attend.

I give detailed guidance on technique in my companion volume, *2-4-6-8 How Do You Communicate?* and in later chapters, so I shall only touch lightly on them here. The techniques you need to develop start with **platform presence** and end with your **exit line**. In between, you need structure and the skills of **delivery**, such as **vocal variety, passion, conviction, pitch, pace** and **pauses**.

Platform presence is about taking charge from the very moment you are visible to your audience. After all, would you want to listen to someone who looks unimpressive, dresses badly and fidgets nervously? A friend of mine was working with an expert in a well-known communication technique, and she asked me and one or two other mutual friends what we thought of the speaker. Quite separately we all said the same things: although he clearly knew his subject thoroughly, he looked as though he had slept in his suit and his speaking style was so poor that we would not wish to be guided by him in anything, let alone something as influential as that communication technique.

My purpose in this chapter, and in this book, is not to help you to deliver a good speech. It is to encourage you to deliver a GREAT speech! So I shall not concern myself with whatever may be good enough, but rather with what takes you to the highest level you are capable of reaching.

You must therefore listen critically to the sound of your own voice. Your voice is the vehicle for your message, and it needs to help and not hinder the communication. You must have a tape recorder that plays back a faithful reproduction of the way you sound. Initially, you may not like the way you sound when you play back a recording, but you can change that. You can change the way you sound, and in Chapter 8 I offer you some ideas on how to do so.

You must also **make every speech a performance**. Use your full vocal range, pause for effect, and to allow your listeners to take in what you have just said, vary your pace and your volume, and speak with the animation that your conviction demands. Above all, speak *to* your audience, not *at* them.

◆ Believe in your message and in the benefit it brings to your audience.

◆ Lift their spirits and their energy, so that they want to adopt your ideas, but do not neglect to tell them what they can do about them.

◆ End with a bang.

Let them leave the room with your core message ringing in their ears. Remember that the purpose of a great speech is to bring about some change in their thinking, attitude or behaviour.

One last thing: make the speech your own. Tell your own stories, or acknowledge the source if you use someone else's story. In one issue of *Toastmaster* magazine, **Paul Evans** (author of *Step By Step to Unforgettable Messages*) wrote of an occasion when he was listening to 'one of the best speakers on the circuit'. He admits to being mesmerized for a time, and then he became uneasy. This is what he wrote: 'A couple of his illustrations sounded familiar. He related the stories in the first person, but I knew the individuals to whom the events occurred. Changing a few of the details, he plagiarized a story in front of 2,000 attendees.'

In England, my friend **Paul Joslyn** related a similar tale. A certain speaker told his audience that he had been travelling on a train when two young children were running about, behaving badly. The speaker said he remonstrated with the father, who apologized and said, 'We've just buried their mother ...'. I think you know the story. After the meeting, Paul approached the speaker and said, 'That story wasn't original. It came from a speaker in America.' The man replied, 'But this audience is unlikely to have travelled to America, so they wouldn't have heard the story before.' He was that cynical.

What was the effect on Paul Evans in America and Paul Joslyn in England? They lost respect for the speakers and became sceptical about the rest of their messages. Paul Evans expressed it well, writing, 'No amount of talent can save a speaker who ignores the two unbreakable laws of speaking: the law of character and the law of content.'

The old saying, 'Walk your talk' applies here. Live according to the high principles you propose in your speeches. Be honourable at all times, especially when you think no one else is watching. Who you are will always speak more loudly than what you say. If you are the kind of person you urge others to be, you will be worth hearing.

In summary . . .

◆ **Don't be self-satisfied. Find out how others feel about your speaking.**

- ◆ Let your content serve your listeners' needs rather than your own.
- ◆ Be realistic about your skills: would you pay to hear you speak?
- ◆ Take charge of the platform from the first moment you appear.
- ◆ Work on sounding more interesting (see Chapter 8).

Chapter 3

Introductions are launch pads

In this Chapter:
- ◆ why speakers need good introductions
- ◆ the difference between good and bad introductions
- ◆ what the introducer should never do
- ◆ the purpose of introductions
- ◆ advantages and consequences
- ◆ how to make a ROCKET of an introduction
- ◆ examples.

The **introduction** is an essential part of speechmaking. If you are the chairman of the meeting, or if you are the speaker, you must take hold of the introduction and make it work. All speakers need to know how to make good introductions, both to ensure that they get the right build-up before speaking, and because making an introduction is one of the skills that make a complete speaker.

In this chapter I propose to illustrate bad introductions and discuss why they are bad or inadequate, and how they could be improved. I shall explain why it is important to have a good introduction, and what must be included. Let's start with an example of an introduction that failed the speaker:

> Our next speaker is going to tell us about his
> travels in America and what he found so
> exciting in that country. Michael Steel says he
> often goes there, and he's here to tell us his
> latest adventures.

The chairman then stopped talking and looked towards the speaker, gesturing limply as much as to say, 'It's all yours.' The audience didn't know when to applaud, so as the speaker strode to the front there was a smattering of applause that rapidly died, leaving the speaker high and dry. He had to crank up his audience from cold. So let's consider why this (fairly typical) introduction was less than adequate.

◆ It was too vague about the topic that was to be covered in the speech. 'About his travels' – what kind of travels? Was he a package tourist, an explorer or an historian? Or did he simply go to America on occasion, either on business or visiting friends?

◆ In saying something as meaningless as 'what he found so exciting in that country', the chairman revealed that he hadn't the foggiest notion of the speaker's content, and probably hadn't exchanged more than a couple of words with him before the meeting.

◆ 'He's here to tell us his latest adventures' is a form of words that diminishes the value of the speech.

◆ There was no mention of the speaker's credentials. Why should anyone want to hear Michael Steel talk about America? Does he have some special insight, some particular expertise, some unusual purpose in travelling to America? Why is it Michael Steel is talking, and not someone else?

◆ There was no 'hook' – nothing to grab the attention of the audience and make them want to sit up and listen.

◆ It was not obvious when the introduction was over, save for the embarrassed silence at the end. He should have ended the introduction with the speaker's name, raising his voice.

◆ The speaker was left to create his own first impression, without the benefit of a 'launch' from the chairman.

◆ The chairman did not take his introduction to a climax, nor did he lead and sustain the applause until the speaker was in the position to take charge of the platform.

Now you may be thinking, isn't that rather a lot to squeeze into a brief introduction, and you'd be right. But, you see, there's a lot more to an introduction than you may have thought.

There was a time (and this may have happened to you as well) when I arrived to deliver a keynote address, and the chairman took out his business card, turned it over, and poised a pen over it as he asked me for some information about myself. I said, 'Are you proposing to write my introduction on that card?'

He replied, 'Well, yes. I mean, I only need a couple of brief facts about you, don't I?' He then admitted that he was a last-minute replacement, and that he had no experience of chairing such a meeting. I think he was intending to state my name and occupation, then announce my topic and subside into his seat. I wasn't going to let him. So I sat and scribbled a proper introduction for myself.

He looked astonished that I was writing more than a couple of sentences, but I just smiled at him and handed him the introduction with the request that he read it as I had written it. When he opened the meeting, he suddenly found himself out of his depth. His opening remarks were rushed and uninteresting, and he failed to connect with the audience. In desperation he decided to introduce the speaker (me) and picked up the piece of paper I'd given him. He read it out as I had written it, and his confidence improved visibly. Later he told me it had given him the feeling of how a chairman should sound. He was pleased, and so was I.

Some dos

What should an introduction consist of? It should:

◆ engage the attention of the audience

◆ raise their expectations, but not too highly

◆ launch the speaker

◆ mention his or her name several times

◆ establish the speaker's expertise or qualifications

- state what the speaker will be talking about (speech title)
- be brief
- create a good impression of the speaker.

Bad introductions create bad first impressions

Some don'ts

Here are some things that should be missing from an introduction:

- 'This speaker needs no introduction...'
- 'Without further ado...'
- 'When I asked the speaker how I should introduce him, he handed me this piece of paper, so I shall read it out...'
- 'Let me introduce Jim and his good lady wife, Mary...'
- 'Put your hands together for...'
- 'We are lucky people because we have none other than...'
- 'I've heard he's a good speaker...'

Needs no introduction...

Then why make one? This is just lazy talk.

Further ado...

First of all, it's old fashioned. Secondly, have you considered what it means? Do you really intend to say that it has been a bit of a nuisance talking about the speaker, so let's quit now? 'Ado' means 'difficulty, bother or fuss'. Think of 'Much ado about nothing'.

Speaker gave me this...

This undermines the speaker. It says, in effect, 'I'm not taking responsibility for the good things I'm about to tell you about the speaker' and implies that the speaker is immodest. It also reveals that the chairman (you?) hasn't done his homework. Altogether, it's not very professional. What's more, it is likely to infuriate the speaker, which is not the best frame of mind for starting a speech!

Good lady wife...

The phrase is so cringe-making. Does he have a bad wife as well? Sometimes people say 'good lady' or 'better half'. Don't be one of them. It's a shibboleth that demeans the lady and you as well.

Hands together...

In prayer? It's one of those dreadful clichés that have been popularized by ill-educated game show hosts on TV.

None other than . . .

It's all a bit unnecessary, and reminds me of the introduction song to Donald Duck cartoons, which ends, 'No one (pause) but Donald Duck!'

Heard he's good . . .

Sounds like a challenge. 'Heard he's good, so let's see if it's true!' It places an unfair burden of proof on the speaker, and raises the audience's expectations to an unreasonable level.

What is the purpose of introductions?

For guests/friends

◆ To tell you who they are, giving you their names.

◆ To tell you why they have come (context).

◆ To make them feel welcome.

◆ To allow you to applaud/acknowledge them.

For speakers

◆ To tell you who will be speaking.

◆ To establish their credentials (context).

◆ To warm up or rouse the audience.

◆ To give the speaker a flying start.

For events/topics

♦ To create anticipation/excitement.

♦ To inform – what's it about, why is it important.

♦ To create context – place it on stage.

Consequences of introducing a speaker badly

♦ The speaker has to establish his or her own credentials.

♦ While audience is wondering who he or she is, they aren't listening.

♦ The speaker has to warm up the audience, perhaps losing a prepared opening.

♦ Limp or delayed applause through weak leadership diminishes speaker.

♦ Weak/unimportant speaker reflects badly on your organization.

♦ Audience doesn't know when or if to applaud.

♦ Person being introduced doesn't know when to rise.

♦ Irritation: in speaker, in audience – a bad way to start.

Advantages of good introductions

♦ Good manners.

♦ Evidence of proficiency in toastmaster skills.

- ◆ Creates the right expectations.

- ◆ Properly informs audience: about the subject and speaker.

- ◆ Warms up the audience.

- ◆ Launches the speaker.

How to do it right

- ◆ Consult the speaker beforehand.

- ◆ Obtain only Relevant information for the occasion.

- ◆ Consider your Opening/maintain good Order.

- ◆ Present speaker's Credentials.

- ◆ Give the speaker/guest Kudos.

- ◆ Do it with Enthusiasm.

- ◆ Give Title – speech/speaker/topic.

Let your **ROCKET** *launch* the speaker!

Finish on the speaker's name, with a rising flourish: John (pause) SMITH!

Examples

Example of correct guest introduction

It's my privilege to welcome our guests, and I'd like to introduce each of you in turn. When I introduce you, please stand so that everyone can see who you are.

This evening we have a guest from the United States who is making her first visit to London. Her name is _____ and she is a friend of our President. As this is her first visit to an English Toastmasters meeting, let's give a very warm welcome to_____!

Example of correct session leader introduction

This half of our programme is devoted to practising impromptu speaking. We call it Table Topics, and the session leader is called the Table Topicsmaster. This evening we are fortunate in having _____ as our Topicsmaster. _____ is an experienced Toastmaster, well known for his wit and for the care he takes in preparing for such a session. Before I invite him to lead the session, may I just remind you of the formalities we follow. Would each speaker please remember to shake his hand when you come forward to speak, and again when you finish. Also, it is customary to start by addressing him as Mr Topicsmaster. That said, let us look forward to a stimulating Topics session led by our Table Topicsmaster, _____!

Example of correct speaker introduction

Our next speaker is well known to you all. I won't say he needs no introduction, because it is always a pleasure and an honour to introduce Les King, a man of many parts. He is witty, humorous, and a fascinating raconteur. When Mike Silverman appointed him Area Governor, he said that it was proof that Mike has a sense of humour. Among his many interests is a fascination with computers and with the Internet, which he uses to communicate with toastmasters everywhere. This evening he is going to show us how easy it is to cope with the complexities of the internet. The title of his speech is, 'Talk is cheap, but the net is cheaper.'

Ladies and gentlemen, let's give a friendly welcome to our Area Governor,

Les (pause) KING!

In summary . . .

◆ **Introductions are essential but can help or hinder the speaker.**

◆ **Bad introducers are either lazy or insensitive.**

◆ **Good introductions reflect well on the chairman.**

◆ **Don't hang the speaker out to dry.**

◆ **Toastmasters learn to do it right.**

Chapter 4

Tell us what you know

In this Chapter:

◆ **what audiences want from a speaker**

◆ **meet the Pros**

◆ **how to gain wisdom from others**

◆ **five ways to identify your message**

◆ **when the audience goes 'Aha!'**

◆ **what an idea could be worth.**

Patricia Fripp is a celebrated speaker in America. Originally from Britain, she went to Hollywood as a hairdresser to the stars and graduated to the speaking business, becoming one of the leading lights of the National Speakers Association (NSA), and an expert on what it takes to be a successful speaker. When asked what audiences want from a speaker, she replies, 'Wisdom'. She adds that people want from a speaker what they cannot get from anyone or anywhere else. In marketing parlance, what they want is your Unique Selling Proposition – your USP. That's what distinguishes you from everyone else.

That fact has been repeatedly verified at the annual conventions of the NSA in America and the Professional Speakers Association (PSA) in Europe. One of the most popular sessions is called **Meet the Pros**. Typically, it consists of three sessions of 20–30 minutes each in which a table is hosted by a professional speaker who speaks for half the time on his or her expertise, then answers direct questions for the second half. It is the most direct method of picking the brains of experts and getting answers to the questions that all speakers have, concerning how they could and should accelerate their careers.

Interestingly enough, the host speakers are not expected to be polished, and some of the preferred tables are hosted by speakers' bureau representatives, who are not professional speakers themselves.

◆ **Tell me how to market myself ...**

◆ **Which topics are hot at the moment ...**

◆ **How do I get booked for such and such kind of event ... ?**

Those are the sort of questions that fill the air.

At other tables, people ask:

◆ **How did you go about getting that work ...**

◆ **How do I know if I'm ready ...**

◆ **What can you tell me about the skills/knowledge/ expertise I need ... ?**

The focus is on self-interest, and on how the speaker can help to satisfy that interest. And why not? That's what Meet the Pros is about, and the popularity of the session proves that there is and always will be demand for expertise. Or, to put it more fully, demand for the interpretation and application of knowledge and expertise. People don't just want you to tell them the facts, they want you to tell them what those facts mean to you, and what they could mean for them. In simple terms, they want you to say: 'This is what happened, this is what I learned, and this is how you can apply the lessons.'

Buddhist monk

The all-important question is, where do you derive your wisdom? Do you take the ideas of others and put a spin on it, or do you search your own life experiences for something worth talking about? What if you feel your life has been too ordinary and lacking in the struggles that make up rags-to-riches stories? What if you have always been averagely successful, without the pain of a life-changing experience?

I heard a Buddhist monk from Scotland on the radio speaking about the time he was preparing a talk. On that occasion he also couldn't find any inspiration. He searched Buddhists texts, but nothing touched him. Then he realised that he was looking for borrowed ideas, and he remembered a Buddhist teacher who once said, '**A life that consists of a stream of external events, without a moment's inward reflection, is not only meaningless but also painful.**' Doesn't that sound familiar?

Too often we rely heavily on *what others have done before*. We doubt the value of our own thoughts and look for facts, figures, statistics, and case histories to lend credibility to our message. But *whose credibility* are you establishing if you *stand in borrowed clothes* or hide behind facts and figures?

Relating to your audience

Audiences want you to understand their industry, to relate to their problems, right down to the appropriate scale, and give them stuff they can use. They don't want to have to interpret your message and take the additional step of working out how to apply it to their circumstances. That's your job.

My business partner, **Debbie Swallow,** was asked to address the Independent Footwear Retailers Association (IFRA) at their annual conference. She was anxious about her speaking skills, and wondered if she would have anything worthwhile to offer. I told her to stop worrying because no one knew more about retailing than she did, as she has a family business in stationery, and had rescued it from the brink of collapse. So she decided to talk about that experience – about how the business suddenly ran out of money, and how she had to turn it around urgently and save the jobs of all who worked for her.

The audience loved her. They saw her as one of them. To them she was someone who had encountered the kind of problems they faced every week, and who had taken the necessary practical steps to make things right. The questions they asked her at the end were about the details of what she did, where she raised the cash to keep going, what the bank said, how her suppliers behaved, and how the staff reacted to the bad news. Her answers further convinced them that she was someone they could learn from.

This is how to connect with an audience:

1. **Find out what their immediate concerns are.**

2. **Tell them stories from your own experience that allow them to identify with you.**

3. **Give them ideas and tips they can put to use right away.**

4. **Use language that they can understand and relate to.**

5. **Help them to understand what works and why.**

6. **Direct them to a course of action that will benefit them.**

There are three stages in the change that you bring about in their thinking:

1. The audience agrees to listen to you

Just because you start talking doesn't mean that your audience is listening. You have got to win their attention. Two things will help you get that attention: a **hook** and **credibility**. The hook is the device clever speakers use to dramatize their opening. It could be a story or some unexpected twist on a popular belief, it could even be a piece of theatre with some visual aid.

Credibility comes from your credentials. Your chairman or introducer will tell them who you are and why you have been asked to speak, but you must quickly provide evidence of the expertise that your introduction has promised.

2. The audience goes 'Aha!'

This is when the audience gets what you are driving at. To you it may seem obvious from the start, but the audience is never listening to what you are saying. They are listening for what it means for them.

I was watching an **Oprah** programme one day, and her guest was **Gary Zukav**, talking about how to overcome compulsions. Oprah fed back to him what she understood him to be saying, and there were puzzled looks on the faces of the studio audience. Gary kept repeating his mantra about looking inside yourself. He knew what he meant, but no one else did, until at last he said you need to identify the physical symptoms you feel when you need to act out your compulsion: the tension, the pain, the racing heart. It was only when he actually said 'physical symptoms' that everyone knew what he meant, and there were nodding heads all around. That was the 'Aha!' moment.

3. The audience takes action

Remember, the purpose of your speech should be to bring about change – in the thinking, attitude or behaviour of your audience. When that change takes place, you have succeeded. Your object must therefore be to take your listeners up to the point when they think, 'Yes! I want that!' and then adopt the ideas you have given them. Anything less than that and all you have achieved is a diversion for the duration of your speech. So plan a crescendo for the end of your speech, with a ringing exit line that focuses their minds on your core message.

Identifying your message

There are five ways to identify your message:

1. What's your speech title? Does it carry a sexy attraction that would persuade people to pay to hear you speak, and is that what you really want people to hear and to know?

2. Would you pay to hear you speak on that topic?

3. What's the sub-title of your speech? Does it describe the essential ingredient of your topic?

4. What do you want people to carry away in their minds and in their hearts long after you have finished speaking?

5. If someone approaches a member of your audience, after you have finished, and asks what your speech

had been about, what would you like the answer to be?

Ideally, all five tests should come up with the same answer.

Successful professional speakers concentrate on a very small number of topics, maybe as few as two or three. They make themselves expert on those topics, creating a niche for themselves, so that when you think of those topics you think of them, and when you think of them you think of those topics. They achieve that by concentrating on what they want to say about that topic, not on delivering a dissertation on the topic itself.

What's an idea worth?

What's the value of your speech? You will be delivering an idea that belongs to you, and which you now want to share with others, but is it worth anything to them? You may wonder what an idea may be worth. It's something that you know, and it may be part of your way of life, but is it worth much when others adopt it and change their lives accordingly?

Here's a simple example to illustrate the cumulative benefit of a small change. Liken the change to a one pound coin, and suppose the value of the change you bring about in someone else's life is worth as little as one pound. Not much, you might think. And let's consider, for the moment, that there was no additional, cumulative benefit, just the initial benefit, repeated day after day.

Now, suppose your parents had put aside £1 on the day that were born, and continued to add £1 every day of your life until you were able to take on the responsibility yourself, and you added £1 every day until you reached the age of 70 – three score years and ten. How much money would you have? The answer is £25,567.

But suppose you had invested the money?

◆ At 5 per cent interest you'd have £250,000.

◆ At 10 per cent interest you'd have £3 million.

◆ And at 20 per cent interest you'd have ONE BILLION POUNDS!

So an idea that adds benefit to someone else's life, and improves their existence by even a few percentage points, can be said to be worth millions.

Your starting place

So, to summarize, when you start preparing a speech, *ask yourself three questions*:

1. **What do I want to say about this subject?**

2. **What do I think about it?**

3. **What do I want my audience to think or do about it?**

Do that and your speeches will have focus, they will be different, distinctive and special. To make a worthwhile speech you must dare to be different. You must be prepared to say, 'This is what I think. And this is what I want *you* to think!' You *do* have something to say, and we want to hear it. If it changes our lives, it could be worth a fortune.

The **essential ingredient** that makes the difference between an ordinary speech and a worthwhile one is **the part that is you**.

– It is the flavour and the colour that you impart to your message,

– it is what happens when you do not go where the road leads you,

– but go where there is no path and leave a trail for others to follow.

Let me offer you these words from the poet **Robert Frost**:

> Two roads diverged in a wood, and I
> Took the one less travelled by,
> And that has made all the difference.

In summary . . .

◆ **Everyone wants to know how someone else succeeded.**

◆ **Stop looking outwards: the answer may lie within.**

◆ **Relate to your audience's concerns.**

◆ **Check that *you* think your message is good enough.**

◆ **An idea that adds daily benefit could be worth millions.**

◆ **The most important part is the part that is you.**

Chapter 5

Developing your topic

In this Chapter:

◆ **becoming an expert**

◆ **having something to say**

◆ **the difference between information, knowledge and wisdom**

◆ **oratory without substance is not enough**

◆ **substance without vision is boring.**

Step out and stand out from the growing crowd of lookalikes. *Tom Peters*

Becoming an expert

One of the most pressing concerns of those wishing to develop a speaking career is 'What shall I talk about?' The amateur is likely to say, 'I am a good speaker. Give me a subject and I'll make a speech on it.' That approach has three fundamental flaws in it:

1. **It betrays a lack of personal expertise.**

2. **It assumes that oratory matters more than substance.**

3. **It fails to recognize that no one will book (and pay for) such a speaker.**

There is a world of difference between the professional speaker and the amateur.

◆ The amateur wants applause, and practises until he or she gets it right.

◆ The professional wants recognition as the expert, and practises until he or she cannot get it wrong.

Both are self-centred, in a way, but the professional offers substance, while the amateur might only offer froth.

That is not to say that amateur speakers do not offer value. Nor is it to say that they are not very good, and even better than some professional speakers. I am talking about their focus. **The professional speaker is paid to speak and must therefore provide value for the fee.** If the speaker is a celebrity, the value is provided just by turning up, because that is what puts bums on seats. The very fact of the speaker's celebrity – as a sports personality, a pop star, a politician or a movie actor – is what attracts the audience. They want to be able to claim, 'I met so and so. Heard him speak.'

However, most professional speakers are experts first, celebrities second. People like **Sir John Harvey-Jones** and **Charles Handy** have things to say that people will pay money to hear. Even motivational speakers like **Les Brown, Peter Legge** and **Mitchell** have messages of value to impart. They have an exceptional outlook on life, and advice on how to acquire that outlook to benefit your own life, and they have the capacity to raise your spirits and inspire you to do things differently. That is their expertise. They know what works and why it works, and they keep their messages fresh.

The question is, how do you become an expert like them?

1. Personal expertise

What do you know? What do you know more about than anyone else? What do you know inside out and back to front? That's a good place to start, when you are trying to discover your own topic.

What is an expert?

Experts are those who are so closely identified with their subjects that when you think of the subjects you think of their names, and when you think of them you also think of their subjects. Experts have:

♦ **knowledge across the whole breath of their subjects**

♦ **made specific and unique contributions to their subjects**

♦ **gained a reputation in their industry or profession**

♦ **knowledge that others value (and would pay to receive).**

Someone who has read a couple of articles from the Internet is clearly not an expert, and nor is someone who has researched and given a single talk on his or her subject. It does happen, of course, that some speakers can successfully pass themselves off as experts in limited areas, but it's not a practice I would recommend.

Even having detailed knowledge is not enough for a speaker. You need to have **a point of view** about that knowledge. What does it mean? How can your listeners use it? Is it worth paying to hear it?

Remember that knowledge is much more than information. You can get information from a book. You can give people facts until their eyes swivel in their heads, but that will not necessarily change their thinking. That is more likely to leave them shaken than stirred.

The dictionary defines knowledge as 'an understanding gained through experience or study'. The key word there is 'understanding'. It enables you to create a filter though which you can pass the facts, to colour and explain them and make them relevant to a particular situation.

The way I construct the sequence is this:

    information → understanding → knowledge
    knowledge → applied → verified → WISDOM

2. Oratory v. substance

As I said earlier, many an amateur speaker believes that it is enough to be a powerful or dramatic speaker. It is not enough.

Some people in Europe say that American inspirational speakers play on the heartstrings of their audiences and succeed in making them want to do things differently. But in the cold light of the next day, the listeners realize that they haven't been told how, and that they have been swept up on a wave of oratory rather than substance.

Northern Europeans such as the Finns and Germans are at the other extreme. They plunge straight into facts, figures and information, because that is what they have been conditioned to believe is irrefutable. They have less regard for the speaker's opinions than for the material evidence presented to them. It may be said, therefore, that they are much less impressed by oratory than by substance.

So what is the poor speaker to do, faced with the choice between speaking with passion and filling the speech with facts? I take my guidance from a favourite saying of a man I once worked for. He used to say: *'Always tell the truth, but make the truth fascinating!'* It's a way of saying, 'Deliver the facts, but liven up their presentation.'

> I'm not going to sit on the fence, because that's how you get splinters where you may not want them. So let me state my own position. I believe that **people will pay for knowledge**, but they will not pay a second time to be bored. You must deliver substance, but you need to develop the skills to make your speech interesting. Even Finns and Germans have emotions, and they buy the

things they want rather than only the things
they need, just like the rest of us. That means
they are susceptible to having their
heartstrings pulled, even if you have to explain
why you are doing it.

3. Who is the piper, and what is the tune?

There is a traditional saying that *he who pays the piper
calls the tune*. Does that mean you should deliver a
speech that the client or agency asks you to give? The
answer is – certainly, if you know enough about it, but
not otherwise. Don't be tempted to take on an
assignment that could expose you as a fraud. Not only
will you risk your entire reputation, but you may not
even get paid if your performance is poor.

Speakers' bureaux have repeatedly reminded me that a
client depends on the bureau to recommend a speaker
to match the requirements of the occasion. If the bureau
recommends you and you perform badly, you may lose a
single fee, and perhaps something of your reputation,
but the bureau can lose the client, and all the business
that the client places. So why should the bureau take a
chance?

Whoever pays your fee is entitled to tell you what they
are expecting, and you need either to deliver that or tell
them you cannot do so.

Bureau owners are quite blunt about it. They ask, 'What
can you offer that I can't get from a better known

speaker? What expertise or twist can you offer that is worth my client's fee, and worth risking my relationship with that client?' Most wannabe speakers cannot answer the question, but you will need to find an answer if you want to break into professional speaking.

Let me turn to how you can achieve that. The first step is to identify your topic or topics, and let me stress that you should limit yourself to one or two, or three at the most. I don't want to be prescriptive about it, but too many speakers find themselves disqualified from consideration because they list six or seven speeches, all on different subjects, and expect to be regarded as experts or specialists in all of them. Resist the temptation. **Specialize!**

Here's how to discover if you are entitled to call yourself an expert. Make sure no one else is around, shut the door, and put a mirror in front of you. Then answer the following questions as truthfully as you can:

1. What subject do you know most about?

2. Do you know more about it than anyone you know?

3. Could you write an article on it in the leading trade journal?

4. Could you write a book on it without doing a lot of research?

5. Would you be prepared to appear on a TV programme on that subject, right now, and take questions from a live audience and Jeremy Paxman?

6. Have you anything to tell people about the subject that they can't get from a book?

7. Have you ever given a talk about it to an audience you didn't know?

8. Would you pay to hear your views on the subject?

It's not a comprehensive test, nor is it based on anything scientific, but if you can honestly answer 'Yes' to all or most of those questions, you are probably entitled to call yourself an expert. You should therefore develop your answer to question 6 and write a speech and/or an article on it.

Two kinds of experts

In broad terms, there are two kinds of expertise in public speaking:

a. substance

b. vision.

A. Substance

This relates to the factual content of your speech(es). You are a substance speaker if you deliver facts, figures and information. You know things, or you've done something that others have not, or had some unique experience. Examples of substance speakers include:

◆ **explorers** who talk about where they've been, what they did there and what they discovered

- **business gurus** who have developed new techniques

- **entrepreneurs** who have started new enterprises

- **heroes** who have done something extraordinary

- **experts** in techniques such as mind mapping, accelerated learning and NLP

- **teachers, lecturers, trainers**, especially in technical subjects.

If you are such a speaker, your role is to inform and instruct your audience, so it is important for you to:

- **Keep up to date:** you are regarded as an authority in your subject, and you can rapidly lose that status unless you know the latest thinking and research findings.

- **Prove what you say:** you must be able to back up any claims you make by providing the evidence, not only when asked, but as you present, because the kinds of people who come to listen to you will expect that.

- **Present interestingly:** remember that facts and figures can be difficult to take in and retain, even for people who are interested in, and knowledgeable of, your subject, so make your presentations visually interesting, with the use of well-designed visual aids.

- **Interpret your information** for your audience: they can get the plain facts from books or other sources. What they want from you is *your* take on the subject – what *you* think about the information, and what you want them to think and understand about it.

B. Vision

This is about your approach to events and life in general. You are a visionary speaker if you see the bigger picture, if you project how to learn lessons from significant events, large or small, if you have the sort of mind that sees how to get the desired result. Examples of visionary speakers include:

◆ **Facilitators** who chair conferences or workshops and guide other experts in arriving at a shared goal.

◆ **Motivators** who share some life-changing experience and show how they (and you) can learn the lessons inherent in that experience.

◆ **Counsellors** who help you to find your own solutions within yourself.

◆ **Business advisers** who can show you how to position your business differently in a crowded market.

◆ **Inspirational figures** who can lift your spirits and make you want to conquer new worlds.

◆ **Self-development coaches** who can give you a greater vision of yourself.

These speakers are less concerned with technique than with attitude or outlook. As someone once said, the difference between stumbling blocks and stepping stones is the way you look at them. Visionary speakers help you to see events as stepping stones rather than as stumbling blocks.

Whichever type of speaker you happen to be, you need a sense of purpose. You need to make yourself aware of what you have to offer. You need to look within yourself and focus on the message you have to impart. Ask yourself:

◆ What do I know that others will want to know?

◆ How will they benefit from knowing it?

◆ What would I like them to do when they have heard my message?

If you had only 30 seconds to tell them something – anything – what would you say? I have found that many people don't know what they know. They don't realize that they have knowledge that could be applied outside their own area of expertise. Let me give you an example of how I helped a friend to develop a powerful professional speech.

Evelyn is an expert in medical informatics. It was the subject of her masters degree. Because it concerns the use of computer technology to maintain patient records in hospitals, Evelyn thought she could speak about it only to medical audiences. One day I came across the story of a child who died in hospital because the doctor did not read his notes (they could not be found), guessed incorrectly, and prescribed the wrong medication. Evelyn said the case was not an isolated one, and as her anger grew I could hear the passion that had driven her to select that subject for her masters degree.

I then asked her, 'What's the lesson to learn from that episode?' and she replied, 'We need to have the right information readily accessible.' With a little prompting, she added, 'We also need to learn from what has gone before, so that we can make the right decisions in the future.' I said, 'Isn't that as relevant in business as in medicine?' She agreed. A little while later, she said, 'It's just as true in our daily lives. Just as relevant for individuals as for doctors and business managers.' She had her speech.

This was the process:

1. What did she know in depth? (Informatics.)

2. What benefits did it provide? (Avoiding incorrect medication.)

3. What was the underlying principle? (Learning from what went before, and having the right information readily available.)

4. Was that relevant to business as well? (Yes, to avoid bad decisions.)

5. Was it relevant to individuals as well? (Yes, to allow us to grow and develop, and not repeat the mistakes of the past.)

You can do something similar with your own area of expertise. Step back from the detailed technicalities that may apply only to medicine or manufacturing or economics or whatever you specialize in, and identify the underlying principle that could be applied more generally. Draw a parallel.

In summary . . .

◆ First decide what you know most about.

◆ Specialize in one aspect of your subject.

◆ Become an expert in depth.

◆ Have your own point of view . . .

◆ . . . but meet the expectations of the meeting planners.

◆ Deliver a vision of what might be.

◆ Show them the path and how to get there.

Chapter 6

Structuring your speech

In this Chapter:

- making it easy for your audience to follow you
- how people listen
- preparing your speaker's notes
- some structures that always work
- a sequence to follow.

One of the oldest adages in speech-making is:

- **Tell them what you're going to tell them.**
- **Tell it to them.**
- **Tell them what you've told them.**

It may be old hat but it's sound advice. However, I'd like to approach the subject of structuring your speech **from a different angle**. I'd like to discuss what happens in the minds of your listeners as you speak, and work backwards from that to the right kind of structure or organization.

Let's start with the main points you should consider when you start to prepare your speech or presentation:

1. Who is your audience?

2. Why are they there?

3. What do you know that they want to hear?

4. What result do you want to achieve?

5. What is your core message?

6. Which aspect of your subject are you going to cover?

7. How will you help them remember what you said?

8. How do people listen?

There may be other considerations, but let's stick with these for now. In fact, let's start with the last point.

How do people listen?

People hear what they want to hear. I once listened to a dialogue between two people who started from positions that were diametrically opposed to each other. **Person A** was supposed to be instructing **Person B** in something. He explained it clearly, but Person B, who disagreed with what was being said, fed it back incorrectly. Person A (the instructor) then explained it differently, but Person B (the pupil) fed it back again incorrectly. **Each time Person A explained it differently, he moved a little closer to Person B's position**. The latter used different words in his feedback, but his position never altered. Now remember, Person A had the right information, and he was the instructor, but Person B could not hear anything except his own point of view, and strange as it may seem, Person A allowed himself to adopt the wrong position, simply because he was trying to connect with his pupil. By adopting the terminology of his pupil, the instructor involuntarily adopted the thinking as well.

Time without number I have heard people say, 'Yes, but ...' as a prelude to appearing to agree, but actually disagreeing totally. When people say, 'I hear what you say' what they really mean is, 'I don't agree with you.' People hear what they want to hear, and will distort what has been said to make it fit their preconceptions.

Speakers need to be aware of this. Almost inevitably their words will be used to prove both sides of an argument, if their topic is a controversial one. This imposes the **first** requirement of speech preparation:

1. Address an important concern of your listeners

The point is: relevance. People usually want their own ideas reinforced, or, if you are offering some new approach, they want you to tell them how it relates to their present position. They want a clear path from where they are to where you want them to be.

That imposes the **second** discipline:

2. Construct a skeleton outline of your speech, consisting of main headings and subheads

◆ **Write it down.**

◆ **Visualize and memorize it.**

Do two things with that outline:

1. use it as your aide memoire when you deliver your speech

2. transmit it to your audience, checking that they have received it well.

It's very interesting how an audience will actually receive what you carry in your mind. If your thinking is jumbled, and your approach is linear, so that you start here and go on until you arrive there, they may listen politely, but they will retain very little.

My economics lecturer at university was a certain **Fr. Mali,** who had been to the London School of Economics. I don't know if he had learned the technique at LSE or made it up himself, but he used to prepare his lectures as headings and bullet points, which he reproduced on the blackboard as he proceeded with the lecture. By the end of the lecture he had put on the blackboard the very notes he had prepared. I also had it in my notebook and in my head, and did not need to do any further work because the outline was clear and logical, I understood it, and I had it for reference if necessary. Really effective.

Remembering that we are working backwards, let's consider the **third** discipline:

3. Limit yourself to one aspect of your subject

It's a common fear that you may not seem impressive enough unless you shower your audience with knowledge. Many a speaker (too many, in my view) will attempt to project a complete dissertation on their topic in the 30 or 40 minutes they have.

Ask yourself these two questions:

1. How long did it take you to become the expert you are?

2. Can your audience, in 30 or 40 minutes, become as expert as you?

Clearly it's not possible, so why try? Focus, instead, on one main message, one aspect of your topic, one new way of looking at things, and make your case plausible. For example, if your speciality is computers, don't cover how computers work, how they developed, their multiple uses, the difference between operating systems and software programs, and so on. Just concentrate on, for example, how computers can help us to manage our crowded diaries, or how they can save us time, or how they can be used to develop and maintain an effective database. The other advantages of computers will be either implicit or irrelevant.

The main thing is, what do you want them to remember and apply? Which leads us to the **fourth** discipline:

4. Write down your core message and refer to it constantly

The core message is a single sentence that summarizes your speech or presentation and states your main purpose. That last bit is most important: you must have a purpose that links your passion with the value or benefit that your listeners will derive. Both must be present for it to be meaningful.

For example, you may have a passion for collecting newts, but unless you are addressing other newt fanciers, what value can you possibly add to people's lives by disclosing how newts socialize? By keeping your written core message in front of you, as you prepare your speech, you will be reminded not to include facts that do not add value to the listener, nor serve your core message. One good test of the value of a piece of information is to ask the question, '**So what?**' Alternatively, as you make a claim or statement, ask, '**Which means that ...?**' and go on asking that question as you dig down to each new layer.

Why do you need to do that? Because you need to be focused on the **fifth** discipline:

5. Decide at the start what result you want your speech to achieve

If you do not have such a purpose, your speech will be no more than a transient entertainment, an ephemeral interlude in your listeners' lives. Would that be good enough for you?

If you don't have an objective or a target, what can you expect to hit?

The target must, of course, be related to the needs of

the audience, and why they have turned up to hear you speak. Bound up with that is the reason why you were the one selected to speak, whether you selected yourself or someone else invited you to speak.

That brings us to the **sixth** and final discipline, before tackling the organization of your content:

6. Only deliver material that is of vital interest to your listeners

We've come full circle to almost the starting point, which was to answer the famous question, 'What's in it for me?' or WIIFM, for short.

Structure

There are several valid ways to organize your material, and you may have your own preferred way. To save you time and mental energy, here are three ways that always work. They are developed in greater detail in my other book, *Blank Page to First Draft in 15 Minutes.*

1. Past/present/future

Give the background first, showing how it led to the present (unsatisfactory?) situation, and then consider the options available in the future. It's an easy structure to follow, whether for a prepared speech or impromptu speaking.

2. Problem/cause/solution

For clarification, state or re-state the problem you are
examining, then take a look at how it came about,
making sure you create a clear causal link. Finally, offer
the options available, before making a recommendation.

3. PREP

This stands for Position, Reason, Example, Position. You
first state what your position or opinion is, explain why
you hold that view, illustrate it with an example that
proves your point, then repeat your position. 'This is
what I think ... here's why ... here's an example of what
I mean ... that's why I think as I do.'

Main points

How many points should you include? As I said earlier,
don't try to deliver the encyclopaedia or to make the
definitive statement on the topic. That would be a waste
of everyone's time, and your audience will never be able
to take it all in, let alone remember what you said.

Limit yourself to **three main points**. No matter how
many points you actually want to make, group them into
three distinct strands, all pointing to a single message. A
speech is not a lecture, nor is it a condensed course of
instruction. Its purpose is to enlighten, inspire or
persuade people to think or act differently because of
one powerful and clearly expressed message.

◆ One message.

◆ Three strands of thought, e.g. past/present/future.

A word about the facts you select and the way you express them. Initially, brainstorm to collect as many ideas and facts as possible. Do not exclude anything. Then cherry-pick the most interesting ones, the ones that make people gasp in surprise, and link them to your message – but only if they are relevant. For example, it may surprise people to hear that a flea can leap 200 times its own body length, developing an acceleration of 200 gravities – the equivalent of a man leaping over a skyscraper. But so what? If it is not relevant to the thrust of your speech, it will only confuse your audience, who will wonder why you mentioned it.

Only the other day I was coaching a very clever man who had devised an interesting presentation on leadership, and he had based it on the true-life story of Shackleton. He even had several video clips from the Kenneth Branagh film about the explorer. One clip showed Shackleton taking decisive action to dismiss two crew members who had gone AWOL in Buenos Aires. 'Interesting,' I said, 'but what's the point you are making with that clip?'

My client said it demonstrated Shackleton's ability to be ruthless when necessary. I then asked, 'But why would your audience of managers care or need to know that about Shackleton? How is it relevant to their needs?' He then pointed out that, when placed alongside a clip showing Shackleton's sensitivity and empathy, it illustrated the man's flexibility. 'The lesson,' he explained, 'is that a manager cannot succeed with only one style of management. He needs to adapt his style to the person and the situation.' I said, 'Now you're talking!'

Your listeners should not be made to translate what you tell them. This is what some speakers expect their listeners to do:

♦ take in what's being said

♦ link it to what went before

♦ understand its relevance to the talk's message

♦ work out its relevance to themselves

♦ decide how to put it into practice

♦ calculate the benefit to themselves, etc.

All that while they are still listening to the speaker. Try listening to the news on TV while reading a newspaper at the same time. It's not easy. So don't impose that task on your audience. Always do the translating for them. Tell them what it means and how it applies to them and how they can put it into practice, and use terms that make pictures in their minds. Abstract concepts make no pictures unless they are related to something concrete, and preferably unusual.

Sequence

Here's a potted guide to the kind of structure or sequence you might follow:

1. **Hook.** Open with some unexpected or startling statement that will grab the attention of your audience and make them gasp. Make it relevant.

2. **Agenda.** State your theme and how you intend to tackle it. People need to know where you are going.

3. **Three main points.** Develop *three* main points, illustrating each with stories or case studies if possible. These could be past, present, future, for example.

4. **Transitions.** Include links between the points to let people know when you have finished with one point and are about to start the next one. An example would be: 'So much for the problem and its causes. Let me now turn to the options that are available to us and see how we can solve the problem.'

5. **Summarize** in outline, e.g. 'Let me remind you of the real problem we face. I talked about how it came about, and showed that the conditions that created the problem are still with us. I stressed that we must first remove those conditions before we can make things better. I then offered you three options, three choices for the future. Option One amounts to very little change, Option Two is too costly, and Option Three offers the best prospects. It's the Option I recommend.'

6. **Action plan.** Tell people what they need to do as a result of what you have told them. Tell them the next step. Example: 'Option Three is attractive, but it won't happen on its own. We must make it happen. We must throw out the old and bring in the new.

Not gradually, not next year or next month, but today and tomorrow and next week. You can start the process with the very next order you place.'

In summary . . .

- ◆ **Start by thinking about who will be in your audience.**
- ◆ **Understand that people hear only what they want to hear.**
- ◆ **Construct an outline to help you remember the sequence.**
- ◆ **Limit yourself to one aspect of your subject.**
- ◆ **Use simple three-step structures.**
- ◆ **Follow a checklist that starts with the hook and ends with an action plan.**

Chapter 7

The language you use

In this Chapter:
- **how the spoken text differs from the written word**
- **how to make it easy to say what you write**
- **meet your listeners half way**
- **help them to make mental pictures**
- **ideas with energy**
- **make memorable phrases**
- **how transitions can keep your audience on track.**

Every once in a while I come across a phrase that says exactly what I have in mind, with all the economy and beauty of poetry, and if it comes from someone else, I borrow it – but acknowledge the source. Just as I was about to start on this chapter, I read one of those phrases, and I'd like to share it with you. It came from **Peggy Noonan**, speechwriter to US presidents. She said, 'You must be able to say the sentences you write.' So simple, yet so profound. If you remember that sentence every time you sit down to write a speech or presentation, you'll make a big improvement.

Joan Detz is another speechwriter, and she says, 'Speeches are meant to be heard, not read. Write for the ear not the eye.'

My own aphorism on the subject goes like this: 'The text that's written to be said is different from the text that's written to be read.'

In this chapter, therefore, I shall focus on:

◆ **language**

◆ **rhythm**

◆ **oratorical devices**

◆ **transitions**.

Language

Let's consider how you can couch your speech in the right kind of language. It must have these characteristics if it is to work as the vehicle for your thoughts and ideas:

1. **It must be your own.**

2. **It must be easy to speak.**

3. **It must be easy to understand.**

4. **It must make mental pictures.**

5. **It must have energy.**

6. **It must contain memorable phrases.**

7. **It must have rhythm.**

I shall deal with the last item separately, but let's tackle each of the other points as they fall.

1. Make it your own

Your speech must be as close as possible to your normal
conversational style, minus the verbal crutches, slang and
swearing that might pepper your conversation with
mates in the pub. Otherwise it will sound unnatural and
you will not be comfortable. Not only that, if you use
unexpected vocabulary, your audience will stop listening
to you and start thinking about how incongruous it
sounds.

2. Make it easy to speak

Think about Peggy Noonan's statement that you must be
able to say the sentences you write. Try saying this
sentence out loud:

> If you are faced with a potentially hostile audience,
> and if appropriate, ask the person who invited you to
> indicate the audience's opinion of you and your
> topic, as well as the names of any especially
> troublesome participants.

The individual words are not unusual, but the way they
are grouped together makes the sentence unwieldy. Also,
the meaning is unclear. Is the person who invited you
supposed to indicate something, or have you been
invited to do the indicating? When there is the
possibility of a double meaning, it may cause you to
hesitate in your delivery.

Now try these sentences:

A. The accumulation of material evidence is the primary requirement in advance of the promulgation of the conclusions that derived inductively from the initial revelations.

B. Cost is a large reason for feeling a reluctance to train people despite the increased awareness of the need for training and the agreement in principle that it must be implemented.

Example A is full of cumbersome words that amount to jargon, and there are too many abstract ideas contained in the sentence. It is an outpouring of vocabulary, rather than a piece of communication.

Example B has simpler words but is not much clearer. It is also hard to speak the sentence because it contains several 'backtracking' words such as reluctance/despite/ need/agreement/must. Each of those words forces you to backtrack and check the position of the parties concerned. It is therefore likely to cause the speaker a hesitation or two, and the listener a few more. That makes it poor communication.

3. Make it easy to understand

Remember, you will be speaking at 150 words a minute or so, having thought out what you want to say. Your audience will hear your words just once. At 150 words a minute. Every minute. On and on. Until you stop. 20–30 minutes later. In that time, they need to hear, understand and retain what you have said, linking all the bits together and deciding if they agree with your reasoning first, and then with your point of view. It's hard work being an audience! So why not meet them halfway and make it easy to understand what you are driving at?

4. Make mental pictures

Avoid negative phrasing and abstract terms. They do not make pictures in the minds of your listeners.

Close your eyes and *do not think of chocolate!* What did you think of? Chocolate, of course. There is no picture for 'Do not', so you get the opposite result if you use negative phrasing. Similarly, abstract terms are harder to take in because they cannot easily be visualized. Consider the difference between these two:

> He was always busy, persistently acquiring knowledge and modifying his behaviour according to the mores of each new discipline, and benefiting from them in the process.

and

> Like a tireless bumble bee sipping nectar from flower after flower, he soaked up knowledge from every possible source, growing and developing as he did so.

5. Give it energy

Since the purpose of your speech must be to bring about change in the thinking, attitude or behaviour of your listeners, you must be persuasive, and that can only be achieved if you speak with energy. Your choice of words must reflect that energy. You cannot expect to achieve your purpose if your words imply, 'Here it is. Take it or leave it.'

Peter Legge is a man who speaks from the platform with considerable energy, and his books are written as if he were speaking. Writing about Rubin 'Hurricane' Carter, who spent 20 years behind bars for murders he didn't commit, Peter says: 'The message I got from Hurricane Carter is that we have an obligation to seize opportunity, even if the rules change – as they certainly did for him, and long ago, for me – even if the ladder of success is sometimes up against the wrong wall, obstacles make us stronger. Lost dreams need not be lost forever. Dare to dream, he said. And by daring, win. We have done that.'

That is the language of a true motivational speaker, a man who doesn't depend on fine words or polished grammar, but rather on the propulsion provided by his purpose.

6. Deliver memorable phrases

We live in the age of the sound bite: a 12-second statement that summarizes or encapsulates a major statement. Demand for instant news and pressure on TV airtime have forced interviewers and commentators to seek the sound bite and leave the details to the printed media. This in turn has educated the listening public to expect pithy, memorable phrases that work almost like slogans. Advertising copywriters have recognized this trend, and they create brand awareness through memorable (if sometimes meaningless) slogans.

◆ **A Mars a day helps you work, rest and play.**

◆ **The tingle tongue taste that's true to the flavour.**

◆ **Go to work on an egg.**

◆ **It's good to talk.**

◆ **Beware of Jeep imitations**.

Politicians' speechwriters are strong on memorable catchphrases such as:

◆ **The pound in your pocket.**

◆ **You've never had it so good.**

◆ **This lady's not for turning.**

◆ **Ask not what your country can do for you. Ask what you can do for your country.**

◆ **An iron curtain has descended across the continent.**

What makes these phrases work is the fact that they all express an idea in a form that the public can understand. They are not merely clever ways with language. They are clever ideas. Find clever ideas and the phrases will take care of themselves.

Rhythm

One of the best known examples of rhythm in a speech is Martin Luther King's 'I have a dream' speech. Here's a snatch:

> I have a dream that one day this nation will rise up and live out the true meaning of the creed: 'We hold these truths to be self-evident, that all men are created equal.'

> I have a dream that one day on the red hills of Georgia the sons of former slaves and the sons of former slave owners will be able to sit down together at the table of brotherhood.

> I have a dream that even the state of Mississippi, a desert sweltering with the heat of injustice and oppression, will be transformed into an oasis of freedom and justice.

> I have a dream that one day my four little children will one day live in a nation where they will not be judged by the colour of their skin but by the content of their character.

> I have a dream today.

You can see and hear the rhythm in the structure of contrasts, 'colour of their skin → content of their character', and in the soaring and swooping of individual words like 'rise up and live out' and 'oasis of freedom'.

Oratorical devices

The same speech deploys another effective device:
repetition. The passage above has 'I have a dream',
which is passive, but the speech goes on with this
passage in the **active voice**:

> Let freedom ring from the snow-capped
> Rockies of Colorado!
> Let freedom ring from the curvaceous peaks
> of California!
> But not only that; let freedom ring from the
> Stone Mountain of Georgia!
> Let freedom ring from Lookout Mountain of
> Tennessee!
> Let freedom ring from every hill and molehill
> of Mississippi. From every mountainside, let
> freedom ring.

As well as repetition and the active voice, there is
alliteration. Listen for the 'k' sound in the first two
lines. Notice the **mental pictures** created by the
adjectives, 'snow-capped' and 'curvaceous', and the use
of mountains as reference points for the states of
Tennessee and Georgia. Note also the reversal in the
final sentence. It not only closes off this section of
repetition, keeping it down to a manageable size, but
leads on to a new section that starts with 'When we let
freedom ring'. It keeps interest high, whereas a longer
list of 'Let freedom ring' cries would lose its impact.

In addition, there is a logical progression from the
demand, 'Let freedom ring' to stating the consequences

with, 'When we let freedom ring'. It drives home the point more strongly.

Language rhythm is of considerable importance in speech making. It raises the quality and effectiveness of a speech above the ordinary, making it memorable as well as enjoyable. The rhythm can be obvious, as in the examples above and the first one that follows, but it can also be more subtle, as the second example below demonstrates:

A. From Neil Kinnock, 1983

If Margaret Thatcher is re-elected Prime Minister, I warn you ...

I warn you that if you have a pain –
When healing and relief depend upon payment ...

I warn you that you will have ignorance –
When talents are untended and wits are wasted, when learning is a privilege and not a right ...

I warn you that you will borrow less –
When credit, land, mortgages and easy payments are refused to people on your melting income.

If Margaret Thatcher wins –
I warn you not to be ordinary.
I warn you not to be young.
I warn you not to fall ill.
I warn you not to get old.

B. From Gideon Hausner, Jerusalem 1961

> When I stand before you, O Judges of Israel,
> to lead the prosecution of Adolf Eichmann, I
> do not stand alone. With me here are six
> million accusers. But they cannot rise to their
> feet and point their finger at the man in the
> dock with the cry *'J'accuse!'* on their lips. For
> they are now only ashes – ashes piled high on
> the hills of Auschwitz and the fields of the
> Treblinka and strewn in the forests of Poland.
> Their graves are scattered throughout Europe.
> Their blood cries out but their voices are
> stilled. Therefore will I be their spokesman. In
> their name will I unfold this terrible
> indictment ...

Transitions

Finally, let's consider transitions. These are the linking passages that tell your listeners you have finished with one section or topic and are moving on to the next one. They are vital. When people are reading a text, they can go back and check the previous passage and see how it leads to the present one. They cannot do that when they are listening to a speech.

You must therefore make it easy for them. Always include regular transitions in your speech and your audience will stay with you to the end. A transition says, 'I've just been talking about such and such, and now it's time to move on to the next point, which is this and this.' Here are a couple of examples:

> So much for history. The historical background
> to our public transport system makes it clear
> why it has been used as a pawn by successive
> governments, and left it bereft of investment
> and under-funded. Let's now consider how
> that approach has created the problems we
> see in our ramshackle trains, our atmosphere-
> polluting buses and our overcrowded roads. It
> is only by looking back over the past fifty years
> that we can understand why we have
> problems in our transport system, and what
> we need to do about them.

That paragraph adds nothing material to the information in the speech, and it could easily be left out, but it does close off the 'past' section of the speech and introduce the 'present'. More importantly, it enables your audience to 'park' what you said about the past and get ready for what you will be saying about the present. It helps them to stay on track with you – Track 150. What I means by that is that people can think at 500 words per minute, but you will speak at, say, 150 words per minute. That leaves their brains with a surplus capacity of 350 words per minute.

When they are not listening to you, they are on Track 350. You need to keep them with you – on Track 150.

In summary . . .

◆ **There are seven characteristics of memorable language.**

◆ **Avoid sentences that could have double meanings.**

◆ **Listen for the rhythm of your language.**

◆ **Make mental pictures and keep them consistent.**

◆ **Make memorable phrases.**

◆ **Use repetition and other oratorical devices.**

Chapter 8

Improving the way you sound

In this Chapter:
- **hearing how you really sound**
- **the breath of life**
- **how to throw your voice to every corner of the room**
- **what makes you sound more interesting**
- **vocal variety.**

'Speak the speech, I pray you, as I pronounce it to you, trippingly on the tongue.' *(Wm Shakespeare: Hamlet)*

Let's consider how to put across the speech you have so carefully researched and crafted. And by the way, you do need to have spent time on preparation before reading this chapter. There's little point in rehearsing a speech that is likely to fail because of insufficient preparation, just as there is no point in reinforcing bad habits.

There's an old saying that 'Practice makes perfect', but I prefer what a certain American speaker maintains: 'Practice makes improvement'. Find the techniques that work for you, understand why they help you to sound better, and go on practising them. An athlete doesn't develop his fitness just once. He goes on exercising to maintain his fitness, so that he can then deliver a high level performance whenever he needs to.

In this chapter we'll concentrate on your delivery, and on developing the techniques that will enable you to make a good impression. Many a business person contacts me shortly before a major speech or presentation and asks for a one-day 'quick fix'. This chapter contains many of the points I cover with them, and you have the advantage of having longer than a single day to practise them, and to refer back to these pages whenever you need to.

There are a number of techniques that could help you to sound better and hold the attention of your listeners. I'll cover more than you will actually need, because I don't know where you might need help. Don't feel you need to apply all the tips in this chapter. Pick any that are relevant to you on this occasion and forget the rest ... until the next time you have to make a speech or presentation.

The points I will cover are:

◆ **how you sound**

◆ **breathing**

◆ **making yourself heard**

◆ **sounding interesting**

◆ **pitch**

◆ **pace**

◆ **pauses.**

How do you sound?

Get yourself a tape recorder. One of those little Sony jobs would be fine. It's about the size of a Walkman and takes a full-sized cassette. If you have a tape recorder with you now, pop in a fresh tape and record yourself reading this passage, then play it back and write down your own impressions.

Did you like the sound of your own voice on the tape? Most people don't like the way they sound, because the tape recorder does not pick up the extra resonance that you hear from your own skull as you speak. So it sounds less interesting to you when you play back the recording. Perhaps even lifeless. However, we can change that.

Now take a deep breath and read the last two paragraphs without taking a second breath, and mark the word at which you had to stop. In a moment I'm going to ask you to do that again, to see if you can get a little further along the line.

Breathing

Perhaps the most boring part of learning to make a speech is breathing. 'I already know how to breathe!' is a familiar cry. My response is that of course everyone knows how to breathe, but under stress, as when you are making a speech, you are likely either to run out of breath or to hyper-ventilate unless you know the correct way to breathe.

Let me take a moment to remind you of a couple of basic facts. Your voice consists of sound made when you push air from your lungs across the vocal folds that are located in your throat, near the adam's apple. The column of air that you project from each lungful is your ammunition clip. If the column is short, you will not be able to fire off many words before you run out of air and need to take another breath.

Take a deep breath now. Did you raise your shoulders? Most people do. Go and stand in front of a mirror and do it again. If you raised your shoulders, you were limiting the amount of air you could take into your lungs. Try this little test: take a deep breath in your usual way, by lifting your shoulders, then start counting aloud until you run out of air. Remember the last number you reached.

Now breathe in deeply by first pushing out your stomach and filling the lower part of your lungs first, then allow your chest to fill out, and start counting again. See if you go past the number you reached with your first breath. That's the right way to breathe.

Put the book down and stand up. Push your chair back and give yourself some space. Make sure you cannot be seen by anyone who might make you feel inhibited. I'm going to take you through a simple breathing exercise that will expand your lungs' capacity, especially if you practise it regularly, and clear your head as well.

- Take a deep breath,

- hold it for the count of two,

- then breathe out completely.

- When you think you have breathed out all the air from your lungs, try to blow out six candles, to really empty your lungs.

Then breathe in again, as deeply as you can. Once again, hold it for the count of two, breathe right out, and blow out six more candles.

Do that for the third time, then relax. If your head is feeling light, it's a good sign, and means your brain is now getting more oxygen than it was getting previously. Stay standing and wait for your head to feel normal again. Still standing, pick up the book again, take a deep breath, and read the two paragraphs once more, starting from – 'Get yourself a tape recorder.' Mark the word you managed to reach. Did you do better? Do that exercise regularly, and see if you improve.

If you do that just before you stand to make your speech, you are less likely to forget your lines.

Making yourself heard

If you can't be heard at the back of the room, people will stop listening and start talking to one another. Even with a microphone some people can't make themselves heard, so let's see what we can do to help you project your voice without shouting. The key to this is **resonance**.

Resonance is achieved by projecting your voice so that it bounces against your front teeth (which are hard) rather than the back of your throat (which is soft). Try this:

Breathe in, then sigh audibly, making a sort of *AAAhhh* sound. It's a soft, teddy bear kind of sound. Now do it again, but this time sigh, 'Happy Birthday'. Think of Marilyn Monroe singing, 'Happy Birthday, Mr President' to Jack Kennedy. That's the kind of voice that does not carry, and if you speak like that you need to consider making a change.

Here's what to do:

Press your forefingers against on your upper lip, and hum. Feel the vibration coming through from your upper teeth and gums. Then say *Yummmmeee yummmeee yummmeee*, holding the *mmmm*, then try to keep the vibration going as you say the *eee* at the end of each word.

When you have mastered that and can keep the vibration going throughout, try saying:

Em-a-na-ting more and more
[Emmmm-aaaa-nnnnaay-tinnngg-mmmaaw-aaannnnd-mmmaaw]

Take your time over each syllable and try to keep the vibration going throughout. Do it loudly and do it softly, but do it often. And always do it before you run through your speech, preferably speaking at a tape recorder that you have placed at the other end of the room.

Sounding more interesting

Wouldn't you like to sound better?

Read or say your speech into the tape recorder. Just a minute or two will do, but say it as you would to a live audience. Now play it back with the sound turned down, so that you can just make out the rise and fall of your voice. Draw a squiggly line, like an oscillograph showing your heartbeats, to illustrate the pattern of your voice. How does it look?

If you do not have a lot of peaks, you should do something about your voice.

Play it again, with the volume at the normal level, and with a highlighter pen, mark on your script the syllables that you have accented. For example, take this sentence from Sample Speech 1. I have marked the syllables that you might hit hardest:

Let me tell you **some**thing about **John**. He was **born** at a time of **man**y changes, **some** of which may have **shap**ed the **way** he has de**vel**oped. As you **know**, he is an **air**line **pi**lot.

Now read or speak the passage again, exaggerating those syllables:

LET me tell you **SOME**thing about **JOHN**. He was **BORN** at a time of **MAN**y changes, **SOME** of which may have **SHAPE**d the **WAY** he has de**VEL**oped. As you

KNOW, he is an **AIR**line **Pi**lot.

Of course, you may accent different syllables from the ones I have marked, because you have a different speech pattern from mine. That doesn't matter. It's the technique that counts. It will make your voice so much more interesting for your listeners, not only on this occasion, but also in your daily life.

Let me briefly touch on the trio of delivery techniques that help your audience to understand all that you are saying, and to enjoy the experience of listening to you.

Pitch, pace and pauses

These are the variables that add variety and interest to a speech or presentation.

Pitch: The key in which you speak, or the main note that is heard. Find the right starting note, so that you sound authoritative and natural, and feel comfortable. Once again, a tape recorder will help you to hear and understand why it is important to speak at the right pitch.

Beware of the tendency to go too high. The larger the audience, the greater the temptation to strain and raise the pitch. Try recording the same passage at several different pitches.

Try switching to a different pitch (usually lower) in mid speech, for dramatic effect.

Pace: The speed at which you speak should also be varied. The ideal speed is between 140 and 160 words per minute. The more energy you put into your speaking the slower you will be, even if it doesn't feel that way. To give the impression of high pace, without losing clarity, hit the consonants of your words, especially the ending consonants.

Pauses: Take your time and do not gabble.

Use the pause ... for dramatic effect .... and to allow your point ... to sink in.

You should pause

◆ ... at the start, to get attention.

◆ ... between main points, as punctuation, and to let your listeners know that you have completed the previous point.

◆ ... before a significant piece of information.

◆ ... before the punch line of a joke.

– Vary the pattern of the whole speech.

– Vary the pattern of each section.

– Vary the pattern of separate paragraphs.

Variety keeps your listeners interested, and signals your willingness to communicate. Are you ready to sound better?

In summary . . .

◆ Don't expect to change the way you sound in a single session.

◆ Never underestimate the power of correct deep breathing.

◆ Develop resonance though humming.

◆ Practise increasing the emphasis on chosen syllables.

◆ Vary your pitch, pace and the use of pauses.

◆ Do you really want to sound more interesting?

Chapter 9

Sounds and pictures

In this Chapter:

◆ **the Mozart effect**

◆ **making pictures when you speak**

◆ **using mental images to help you remember your speech**

◆ **one simple formula for improving your memory**

◆ **the 'image frequency' check on your speech**

◆ **using words that work.**

Earlier I mentioned **Dr Keith Scott-Mumby** and the biology of public speaking. He achieved fame when he proved in court that food allergy could have caused a youth to become murderously violent. He says that if you play the right kind of music to plants, they can increase their absorption of nutrients by as much as 700 per cent. Sounds in the region of 16,000 Hz improve the brain's clarity and lift your level of energy, while music in the 5,000–8,000 Hz range (e.g. Mozart) is highly energizing. Not only that, the **'Mozart effect'** of listening to his music, which is rich in this frequency range, produces an 8 to 10 point improvement in spatial reasoning.

How is that relevant to you as a speaker?

It means there is **scientific evidence of a physical change** brought about by certain kinds of sounds. We already know, from Richard Bandler and other practitioners of Neuro Linguistic Programming (NLP) that matching your vocabulary to your listeners can greatly improve your communication with them.

Keith Scott-Mumby says that it's not only about matching the cognitive process, but it's also about the actual sound produced by the words you choose and the way you speak them. In addition to the meaning of your words, it's *the actual sound of them that makes a difference.*

It goes further than that. There is a link between the words we use and the experiences they describe. We can understand the concept of 'car' because we have the word 'car'. If we did not have such a word, we would have difficulty in grasping the concept. It's as though certain words are more than mere labels, but actually contain the concepts they describe.

Moving on from that, we can choose different words to describe the same thing. However, the choice of words we make will influence the way our communication is received by our listeners. Bandler says, *'The meaning of communication is the effect it produces.'* In practice, **you can improve the receptiveness of your audience quite dramatically**, just by choosing your words with care.

My own view is that we have more chance of making our communication work if we use words that enable our listeners to make mental pictures. Better still if those pictures are coloured with positive emotions. It's about association.

Pictures and remembering your speech

Association works with mental images too. It can help you with remembering your speech and making better contact with your audience. Let me tell you how you can do it. This is based on some ideas I got from **David Thomas**, an International Memory Grandmaster and holder of several memory records.

David says, *'We think in colour. We watch television and movies in colour. And yet we get most of our information in the form of black and white words. Printed words.'* He says we need to turn those printed words into colourful images, and then we will understand and remember the information more readily.

He recommends a simple technique for remembering your speech, so that you are not dependent on notes. **To speak without notes is a liberating experience**. To be able to remember what you planned to say, in the right order, and to have a system that allows you to digress yet never to lose your place ... that can make a huge difference to the way in which you relate to your audience. It adds power to your performance, and is one of the essential ingredients of making an impact from the platform.

First a little exercise

◆ Get out a stopwatch or a watch with a second hand, and time yourself.

◆ Give yourself 60 seconds to read and remember this list of items.

◆ Then close the book and write them down from memory.

Ready?

...

   ...

      ...

video	scissors
hairbrush	barstool
computer	diary
telephone	cat
ballpoint pen	tennis racquet
football	potted plant
toothpaste	photograph
dictionary	mug
letter	passport
filing cabinet	packet of biscuits

      ...

   ...

...

How did you do? What was your score out of 20? Write it down.

Now let me help you to improve that score.

Think of your home, and imagine yourself walking through your home picking out ten places. You could start at the front door or on the roof. You choose. If you have lots of rooms, each room could be a separate location. If you live in a small apartment, you might consider using each internal wall as a location. The only rule is that the locations should follow one another. Thus, front door would be followed by hallway ... then living room ... dining room ... kitchen ... stairway ... bathroom ... etc. If you are using the walls, be sure to go around the room either clockwise or anticlockwise, and do the same in every room. **Visualize the locations**.

Now go back to the list and visualize each item, making exaggerated images and placing each pair in one location. So, we have video and scissors as the first pair, and they will be placed in the first location. For example, you might visualize a large sign on your front door, with a picture of a **black videotape**, with the **brown magnetic tape** spilling out and being cut by a **red pair of scissors**. Use colour and as much detail as you can. Make the images vivid.

If the hallway is the next location, place a **Mason Pearson hairbrush** on a **fancy barstool** in the middle of the floor, so that, as you enter the hallway through the front door, you trip over the stool and just grab the brush as the stool crashes to the floor. Get the idea?

By taking a walk around the ten locations, and introducing some action involving the two items, you will give yourself a better chance of remembering all 20.

It is very important that you use your imagination, create outlandish images, and put in some action if possible. When you have finished, close the book and write down the 20 items again, this time retracing your steps in your mind's eye.

Check the list again. What was your score? I'll bet it was 20/20.

Applying that to speechmaking

Now, how is that relevant to speechmaking? It will help you to remember the sequence of your speech, but it will also encourage you to tidy it up. Here's how.

◆ Write out your speech.

◆ Then, in the margin, draw a line to mark the end of each section.

◆ In this way, break up your speech into 20, 30 or even 40 parts, and

◆ make up an image to illustrate each section.

You may find that in some sections you have too many different little images. That will be a guide to the difficulty your listeners will have in visualizing your messages, so simplify and group your images in pairs, placing them in your 10 locations.

Now make up a short narrative to describe the sequence of images, just as you did with the list of unrelated items earlier.

Too many images can confuse your listeners

Let me take half a step back. In the previous paragraph I said you may find you have too many different little images. Here's an example from one of my own speeches. It's a speech that was well received, but when I tried to make images to help my memory, there were too many. Here it is, with the candidates for images highlighted in bold:

> Have a **fortune cookie.** I wanted to share them with you because I got a fortune cookie once with a profound message. It came with my **Chinese takeout,** and it said, *'Discover yourself and you will have something to declare.'* Wasn't that deep?

> I got food for thought with my **noodles and prawns**. Takeout insight, you might say. Sometimes you can gain insight in unexpected places. I mean, would you expect to gain insight at an **airport**? I did. Let me tell you about it.

> You know how they always seem to ask you the same three questions at foreign airports? Well, this day, when I landed at **Calcutta** in India, the questions seemed related to my fortune cookie.

> The **immigration officer** asked me the three airport questions:

> Who are you?

Why you are here?
Anything to declare?

A **lightbulb** lit over my head. Right then and there, at the airport, I started to discover myself, just as my fortune cookie said I should.

Who am I? Am I who others say I am? The poet, **Robert Burns**, pleaded for the gift to see ourselves as others see us. But me, I'm not so sure. I may prefer the view from here.

Others have called me **cold, arrogant and aloof**. And that was just my **children**. But I did sneak a look back in time, and saw that the pattern for the way I am today was obvious on my first day at **boarding school**.

This is what I call the **'image frequency'** check on your speech. It's the equivalent of the rate at which a film or video changes the image on the screen. Too many changes, switching from scene to scene and from character to character, can be bewildering and will certainly interfere with the viewer's ability to follow the plot.

Divided by a common language?

When I realized that I was creating too many different images, I understood an incident that occurred after I delivered that speech at the Toastmasters convention in Anaheim, California. Note the joke in the last paragraph of my excerpt, about my children calling me 'cold, arrogant and aloof'. It *was* a joke, honest! but I had forgotten that Americans and Brits do not share the same sense of humour. The following day, an attractive American lady stopped me in the hotel lobby and said, *'You know, I loved the opening to your speech, and was with you all the way until you said you were arrogant. Then you lost me because I don't like arrogant people.'*

At the time I thought this was only another example of cultural diversity, but I now think it may have been because I had created too many images for my listeners to take in and follow. She (and perhaps others as well) did not know which bits to take literally, and which bits to take as 'flavouring'.

The creation of images to help your memory could be a useful discipline in keeping your message consistent and easy for your audience to follow. As an old proverb puts it, *One hand washes another.*

Words that work

As speakers we use words, but often do not realize the power of those words. Words have power because they signify thoughts or images, and the most powerful ones are those that create action pictures in the minds of our listeners. Remember, too, that the words we use may have associations of which we are unaware. And now we know, from the work of Dr Keith Scott-Mumby, that the very sounds we utter will generate a physical or biological response, with an emotional effect to follow.

That's something to bear in mind when creating the images that we choose to help us remember our text – how will those images help our listeners to understand and recall what we say? With so much potential power in the words we choose, why would anyone want to choose the wrong ones?

In summary ...

- The sounds we make when we speak produce biological effects in our listeners.
- We can influence their receptiveness by making the right sounds.
- Using words that make pictures will help our listeners to understand what we are saying.
- Mental images can also help our memory.
- Beware of creating confusion by having too many changing images.
- Take the trouble to choose words that work.

Chapter 10

Connecting with the audience

In this Chapter:
- **it's not about the gift of the gab**
- **make pictures that your audience can relate to**
- **being aware of how others perceive you**
- **six types of listeners in the audience**
- **four levels of communication**
- **microphone technique.**

Let me now turn to what happens when you stand to speak. You have researched your speech, planned its structure, polished the text, and now you are ready to deliver your words of wisdom. Before you start, let me say a word about **content** – a word that is more relevant here than in the chapter on your topic. One piece of advice:

> **Beware the temptation to allow eloquence to overtake meaning. Do not mistake verbal fluency for significance.**

Forget about the gift of the gab

Just because the words come easily you are not excused from having to find something (worthwhile) to say.

There are still some people about who believe that public speaking is the preserve of those with 'the gift of the gab'. It's not. It's the preserve *of those with something to say that's worth hearing.*

Politicians are usually people with verbal fluency. They have the gift of the gab and can deliver a speech on nothing at the drop of a hat. However, the current political system works against individual parliamentarians who have something to say. They are obliged to toe the party line, obey the commands of the whips and party managers, follow the lead of the prime minister or president. No wonder men and women with a talent for leadership are reluctant to go into politics.

When people ask me which public speakers I most admire, they always ask if any politicians are on my list, and they immediately shake their heads and admit that they can't think of any worth hearing. Bill Clinton's name often arises as a possible candidate, until I ask what they can remember of his speeches. Nothing. People remember his intensity, his demeanour, his apparent down-home sincerity, but not his message. Not even his catch phrases. And why? Because he is *a prime example of froth over substance.* He may inspire you to want to make change, but he doesn't tell you how. What he does tell you is far from memorable, mainly because he tries to deliver the whole encyclopaedia, instead of focusing on one aspect of the subject.

Make pictures with your words. Remember the brilliant speech Lord Spencer gave at the funeral of his sister,

Princess Diana? Here's a brief snatch in which he describes the way she was:

> To sanctify your memory would be to miss out on the very core of your being – your wonderfully mischievous sense of humour, with a laugh that bent you double, your joy for life transmitted wherever you took your smile, and the sparkle in those unforgettable eyes, your boundless energy which you could barely contain.

Despite the tension of the occasion and the anger with which the speech was delivered, those words conjured up the images of a happy, carefree Diana, free of the pressures and rejections that dimmed her sparkle in the last years of her life. What a wonderful phrase that was – 'your joy for life transmitted wherever you took your smile', and how vivid a picture came to mind when he said, 'a laugh that bent you double'. Those images took us into the narrative, brought us into Diana's daily life, made us feel we'd lost someone we knew.

That was a clever thing to do, and we shall never know if Lord Spencer made that decision himself or if he had a clever speechwriter. Either way, it worked because it used language intelligently, allowing us listeners to march alongside the speaker, so that he was speaking for us as much as to us. It's a process that every speaker should try to master and apply on every occasion.

The time to put it into practice is the moment you are seen by your audience. Many accomplished speakers make it their habit to mingle with the audience as they arrive, shaking hands and introducing themselves. That way they get a feel for the audience and start to make a few friends. We all need friendly faces in the crowd.

When you look at the audience, what do you see?

While it is certainly true that the audience behaves at times as a single entity (call it herd instinct or mob rule or whatever you like), it consists of a number of quite disparate groups, each looking for something different. Chances are, some of them will be a little disappointed, and all of them will be a little surprised. The audience will usually contain:

◆ **blank canvases**

◆ **thinkers**

◆ **feelers**

◆ **doers**

◆ **sceptics**

◆ **enthusiasts**.

When you look at that sea of faces, what do you see? The text books urge you to start by looking for, and at, a friendly face. The temptation is to return to that friendly face repeatedly, for support and encouragement. My own inclination is to concentrate on the unreceptive ones, to remind me to work harder to turn those blank faces into smiles.

Blank canvases are people who have no fixed views on your subject and are waiting for you to inform, instruct or inspire them. To some extent, they probably regard the occasion as a form of entertainment. They start neutral, but want you to give them some reason to line up behind you.

Thinkers want the evidence. They want you to present the big picture, then reveal its component parts. They will follow you step by logical step, and frown at every inconsistency. They add up any percentages you throw out and object if the total is not 100. They want to know your credentials at the start, and want your talk to prove the validity of those credentials. Germanic and Nordic people are like this. So are scientists, doctors, dentists, accountants, financial directors, engineers and others whose work consists of analysis and accountability. For them, precision is all.

Feelers want to know how your speech applies to them. They also want to know the implications of any proposal you make – who will be affected and how, will that be fair, and what is the worst case scenario as well as the best case? They will understand and accept if they can identify with what you say and feel comfortable about it. Their responses will be emotional ones, and they are the ones most likely to cry at a sad story, and to give you a standing ovation if you have succeeded.

Doers want to know how they can put into practice whatever you are proposing. If you speak of an injustice, they want to rise up and change things. They are the optimists, but they are also practical. They will spend quite a bit of time on Track 350, working out how to implement your message, unless you have already worked it out, and take them through it step by step. Unlike the thinkers, they don't need proof before they act, only reassurance that your ideas are sound.

Sceptics sit with their arms folded across their chests, waiting to be convinced. They want you to do three jobs:

1. overcome their preconceptions

2. convince them that your argument is more valid than theirs

3. persuade them to change their thinking or behaviour.

Those who are more obviously sceptical are easiest to turn. Those who are indifferent are the hardest.

Enthusiasts are already on your side. They have read your writings and your website, they know your speeches by heart, they buy your books and tapes, and they will turn up any time your bus comes to town. They want to hear your signature stories – unchanged! – every time. You need them in your audience, so be careful to be consistent and tread lightly on their dreams.

Four levels of communication

Delivering a speech is much more than a one-way street – if it is delivered correctly. There are at least four quite distinct levels of communication:

1. **audience's needs**

2. **your purpose**

3. **substance**

4. **result**.

1. Audience needs

Why are they there? You may be addressing an in-house audience at some large commercial enterprise, or chamber of commerce, or it may be an open seminar with people from all walks of life. What brought them there? Do they have to be there because their employers required them to come ... or did they pay their own money to come and hear you speak? Or is it a celebration of some sort? Whatever the answer, you know that every audience has different needs and you must meet those needs.

No matter what your subject may be, even if it is a speech that you are known for, a speech that you give everywhere you go, your signature speech, you must personalize it to your audience in some way. When I first heard Les Brown speak on tape, it was his speech to the Million Dollar Round Table. Later, I heard him speak on television and in person more than once, and heard the same stories every time, but every time the speech was different. In fact, on that first occasion I thought he had created the speech just for MDRT, because his opening was relevant to the occasion, and in between his stories he drew lessons that applied specifically to that day's audience.

When you spend time considering your audience's needs, and adding in something just for them, you pay them respect. It's the right way to start your communication.

2. Your purpose

There must be a reason why you are giving this speech. You must do much more than transmit information. You must do much more than interpret and filter the information. You must have a personal purpose, a deeper truth that comes from within you and drives you to make the speech. It's not about your ego, it's not about how much you know. It's about something you believe in. It's about your sincerity, and this is what will appeal to the hearts of your listeners more than any number of contrived sob stories.

> When I first met **Mitchell**, a man in a wheelchair with a reconstructed face and hands, I was struck by two things about him: his amazing voice, and his focus. Sure, he has a story to tell about the two severe accidents that could have killed him and left him so handicapped, but he doesn't say, 'Look at me. Feel sorry for me.' Instead, he has a positive outlook and a positive message that he not only believes in, but which he acts out in his daily life. He is self-sufficient, travelling the world on his own, mixing freely with his audiences, giving speeches that are not only moving, but laced with self-deprecating humour. I was going to say he walks his talk, but actually he wheels it!

What's *your* purpose in making the speeches you give? This part of the communication process is about you and the value you get from it. Don't underestimate its importance.

3. Substance

A speech should not be all froth. It must have substance as well. This level of communication is about the argument you devise and the evidence you assemble to support your argument.

At this level you are appealing to the brains of your listeners. Say something they can respect, something unexpected or startling, and back it up with evidence. But be very careful about this. You must get the facts right.

In a bookshop the other day, I picked up a book on public speaking and flicked through it. I thought it looked good, and the ideas it contained were interesting, so I decided to buy it. Just then I turned to the start of the book and saw, to my dismay, that the author, like so many others, had misquoted Dr Albert Mehrabian's infamous statistics on how we communicate: 7 per cent words, 38 per cent tone of voice, 55 per cent non-verbal communication. I immediately lost all respect for the author and returned the book to the shelf.

Those figures would obviously be nonsense even if Dr Mehrabian had actually made the general claim that others attribute to him. But he didn't. His figures referred to a limited experiment involving photographs of facial expressions that were at variance with the spoken words on tape. Clearly, if someone asks you, 'How are you?' and you scowl or wince and say, 'I'm very well', the words would contribute little to the communication, because they would be manifestly untrue. As Dr Mehrabian himself would say (and is apparently saying to anyone who will listen), you cannot then claim that the words *always* contribute as little as 7 per cent of the meaning.

At this level of communication, the facts and the reasoning must be impeccable.

4. Result

The final level concerns the outcome you want. If you accept that your speech is worthwhile only if it sets out to bring about change in the thinking, attitude or behaviour of your listeners, then you must know what that change should be. How will your audience manifest the change? What do they have to do when they leave?

Think of a situation in which someone introduces a new product to you, something that will do wonders for you, enabling you to leap tall buildings with a single bound or design a website in ten minutes flat without special tools, or bring you something else that you would really like to have. You get excited and decide to have it, but the other person walks away without telling you what you must do to get it. Wouldn't you be frustrated?

That's why you must be clear about the action you want your audience to take, and tell them how.

Speaking into a microphone

If the room is big enough to warrant the use of a microphone, and one is available, take it. You will be able to employ more vocal variety, avoid swallowing the ends of your sentences, and you will dominate the room with your voice. I have a powerful, carrying voice, and can usually manage without a microphone. Indeed, I used to pride myself on not needing one, and in my youth I was quite capable of matching a platform speaker who had a mike. It was a macho thing, as though speaking without a mike puts hair on the chest.

These days I take a different view. I believe you should use any aids that are available to you, but that you need to master the appropriate techniques. Time without number I have seen people come on stage from the audience (for example, at awards ceremonies) and lean into the stand microphone, even though they may have been told not to do so. Not only is it unnecessary, but it takes away from your authority and personal presence if you do so.

Microphone technique

Here's how to get the best results when you use a mike:

1. Don't lean into the microphone. Raise it so that you can stand tall and speak as though the mike were not there.

2. Position the mike about nine inches away from your mouth. With an open palm, place the tip of your thumb against your lips, as though playing a trumpet. Your little finger should touch the mike.

3. Find the sweet spot. There is a position where the mike picks up and delivers your voice best. You can hear it yourself.

4. Don't shout. Let the mike do the work for you.

5. Always position the mike below your mouth. If you place it higher, it will block off part of your face, and when you look down at your notes your voice will disappear.

6. Don't get too close, or the mike will pop with every 'p' and 'b' plosion, and hiss on every 'ssss' and 'sssshhhhh'.

7. If you have a strong voice, when the sound engineer asks you to try for a sound level before the meeting starts, deliberately speak with less power than usual, otherwise the sound engineer will set a volume level that's too low, and you could lose impact.

8. Always keep the mike in front of your chin. If you turn to left or right while speaking, imagine that a chopstick links your chin to the mike, forcing you to move your whole body so that the mike is always directly between you and the people you are addressing.

9. If you wear a lapel microphone, get someone to tell you, in rehearsal, if you tend to speak more towards your right or left, and wear the mike on that lapel.

Check that it is firmly clipped in place and that your movement and gestures do not cause any part of your clothing to knock against the mike, as that can be very irritating for the audience.

In summary . . .

◆ Don't confuse eloquence with significance.

◆ Let your listeners *see* what you are saying.

◆ Take account of at least six different types of expectations.

◆ Always make your message relevant to your audience.

◆ Never forget your own purpose in making the speech.

◆ Understand the figures: 7/38/55 before you use them again.

◆ Master the microphone to make the biggest impact.

Chapter 11

Deliver with confidence

In this Chapter:

- ◆ **taking charge of the stage**
- ◆ **think positive or they'll think negative – about you**
- ◆ **how to tap into your personal authority**
- ◆ **communicating with your eyes**
- ◆ **Track 150 and listener's drift**
- ◆ **the power of a visual hook.**

'Confidence is so very sexy'
– *Jack Palance, Mennen aftershave commercials*

This chapter is about your platform presence and the way in which you put your speech across. It's not what you say but the way that you say it that counts. The single word 'delivery' encompasses your personal conviction, vocal variety, gestures, movement, eye contact, confidence and the way you connect with the audience. I have dealt with specific techniques elsewhere in this book, so here I shall concentrate on speaking with confidence – how to gain it and how to project it.

First, a word about the way you come across to the audience.

Don't try too hard – just be in charge

Some years ago, I was in the Anglo-Irish final of the International Speech Contest, and came second. I found it hard to understand the decision then, and still find it inexplicable when I play the video tape of the contest. However, the clue to the result came in a conversation at dinner that night between my then partner and someone who might have been a judge in the contest. She told my partner, 'Phillip wanted too much to win.' I didn't know what she meant by that, but pondered on the remark so that I would understand and not repeat whatever had created that impression.

I decided to play the tape again and concentrate on the way I related to the audience. And then I saw it. It was the opening smile. And the way I mounted the stage.

Just before the contest began, there had been an incident that had made me very tense, and I did not spend any time mingling with the audience, as I usually do. I went into the hall early and sat in the front row, and when it was my turn to speak, I mounted the rostrum at the edge furthest from the contest chairman, so that I walked the full length of the stage before shaking hands with him. Some people minded that. They thought I was being pretentious.

I then turned and smiled (too hard!) at the audience. There was no warmth in the smile, because I was feeling too tense (about the earlier incident), and it looked like a rictus. In contrast, the chap who won didn't bother to smile, he just got up and gave his speech, his manner declaring that he wasn't asking the audience to like him. I thought it was a good speech, even if I thought mine was better.

However, the audience (and, of course, the judges) had already made a decision about me before I opened my mouth to speak. *To them I was a supplicant, pleading to be liked.*

It was very different on a subsequent occasion when someone said he knew I was going to win the very moment I had my microphone clipped on, at the back of the hall. On that occasion I was confident, positive, in charge of the platform. And that's what you must be.

It's not about arrogance. It's about **authority**. Remind yourself:

- **Why it's you that is speaking.**
- **That you are the expert.**
- **That you have things to say that belong to you.**
- **That you are about to deliver some worthwhile benefit to the audience.**
- **That you want to bring about some change in them.**

Let them see your eyes

If you have done any public speaking at all, you will

know the importance of eye contact. It's not about merely sweeping the room with an unconnected gaze, but rather it's about making direct contact with one individual at a time, for two or three seconds at a time, to let them feel that you are speaking to them as individuals, not merely as components of a crowd.

One very significant consideration is the effect of wearing glasses. I wear glasses myself, and I sometimes forget that the audience cannot always tell where I am looking. To give you the right responses, *they need to see your eyes.* On one occasion, I was conducting a workshop for the Professional Speakers Association in London, when I noticed that **Graham Davies**, the celebrated after-dinner speaker, was sitting in the back row looking rather stony faced. Because I knew him well, I ducked my head down, peered directly at him, and said jokingly, 'You can smile if you want to!'

Graham started to smile, but a lady sitting in my line of sight, somewhere between me and him, thought I was addressing her. She immediately apologized and explained why her mind was miles away. Fortunately it gave me the lead to explain what I call **Listener's Drift**. I said that people listen on **Track 150** (see *2-4-6-8, How Do You Communicate?* p. 46), but frequently drift on to Track 350. (See also p. 90)

While they are listening to you, they are on Track 150, with you. But thoughts inevitably intrude, or you say or do something that causes them to stop and think ... and they do that thinking on Track 350. So be careful not to drive your listeners on to Track 350, because they will miss a part of your speech. The more often that happens, the more broken up your message will be, and the less chance you will have of achieving your aim. You therefore need to structure your speech or presentation to loop back frequently (for example, in your transitions between the different sections of your talk), to allow them to catch up. And when you do it, let them see your eyes.

When the workshop ended, Graham and others came forward and said they'd been impressed by that analysis, and had never before thought about the inevitability of listener's drift.

Be a leader

Managers usually have an extended relationship with their team, during which they can build trust and establish the right buttons to press for each person. Leaders don't have that luxury. They have to make an immediate impact. So have speakers.

When you stand on a platform and share your thoughts with a group of people, you are hoping they will accept your ideas and change the way they think and act – after a single hearing of what you propose. That's a tall order. It can work only if you have – and display – leadership qualities.

Your delivery, therefore, should incorporate as many as possible of the following elements:

1. Stage presence: This means looking impressive. Someone once said that public speaking was just 'amplified conversation'. I don't agree. It's much more than that. It's a performance. And for a performance you need to:

- make an impressive entrance,
- command attention while you are on stage, and
- exit with a bang, with the audience wanting more.

How do you do that?

- Plan your opening and closing lines.
- Dress the part.
- Look your terrific best.
- Take your time.

In macho movies, such as Westerns, the hero doesn't rush about when he makes his first appearance. He walks centre-stage, stands still with his feet solidly planted, and he looks around the room, making sure everyone is aware of his presence. Only then does he speak.

You don't *have* to say, 'Get off your horse and drink your milk!' but if you think 'John Wayne' you won't be far wrong.

2. Trust: Picture this. Your audience consists of a number of people who don't know you from Adam. You are about to tell them something new and ask them to accept what you say and make some real change in their thinking, attitude or behaviour. *Why should they?*

The answer is, because **they perceive some benefit** to themselves. However, **that depends on trust**. They must feel able to trust you, and they will only feel that trust if they believe that you genuinely want to help them. It parallels your relationship with your doctor. If you believe that he cares about you and wants to help you get better, you will take the medicine he prescribes. But if you think he just wants to give you pills and get you out of his surgery, you will probably doubt whether you are getting the right treatment for your condition.

3. Multi-layered remedy: Even if you are 100 per cent genuine, you still need to achieve your aim, and that requires the use of persuasive techniques. One such technique is the **multi-layered remedy**. If you ask them to do just one thing, you are more likely to split the audience, with some agreeing with you and some challenging you.

If you give them *several* things to do, such as a three-point programme or a 7-stage process, they are far more likely to accept it whole, as something worth trying. A single proposition can be taken as just a matter of opinion, whereas a 7-stage process sounds as though it has been carefully worked out and verified in live trials.

4. Use a visual hook: You know about the opening hook. It's some device that you use at or near the start of your speech to grab attention. It can be something you say, something you do, or something you show. My preference is for the latter. Showing something is more dramatic and memorable than the other two options.

> At the age of 18 I represented my College in the All-India Inter-Collegiate Debate. There were 22 speakers, 11 on each side of the motion, and I spoke well down the order. While I was awaiting my turn, I could sense that the audience (and judges) must be having difficulty in separating one speaker from another. So when I rose to speak, I walked to the front of the stage and held up my wallet. Within three or four seconds I had total silence and everyone's attention. Only then did I start speaking.

> Oh, and by the way, I won. Many years later, in an Anglo-Irish final of the International Speech Contest, for my hook I did a small sleight of hand trick, making a pound coin appear out of the air and then disappear. I'm sure it helped me to win.

Incidentally, you can use more than one visual hook. Use one at or near the beginning, just to grab attention, and use another one later in your speech to dramatize a particular point. In my mid-twenties, when I was selling management consultancy services, I overcame one prospect's reluctance by scattering banknotes all over the floor of his office. I said, 'Imagine if you could see the cost of wastage and inefficiency in your factory as money being thrown away. Just like this.' I left the cash lying there and carried on talking about the hidden cost of wastage.

People cannot bear to see money lying on the floor, and he was no different. When he finally got the point, I picked up my money. And his order. That was an example of a hook in mid-presentation, and also of being in charge. Be bold, be imaginative, be different. And be confident.

In summary . . .

◆ Let them see you are in charge.

◆ Think 'John Wayne'.

◆ You've got to win the trust of your listeners.

◆ Offer a multi-layered programme for ready acceptance.

◆ Don't be afraid to be different.

Chapter 12

Gestures and movement

In this Chapter:

◆ **how gestures can hinder as well as help**

◆ **making appropriate gestures**

◆ **moving with a purpose**

◆ **how gestures and movement aid understanding**

◆ **10 tips for gestures and movement.**

What's a gesture? Very simply, it's a movement that you make to enhance the meaning of the words you say. Some gestures relate directly to a word or words, others are just there to convey your feeling about the thoughts you are expressing. In this chapter I shall talk about the different kinds of gestures and movements on the platform or stage and how they might either help or hinder the communication process. I shall then move on to how the right kinds of movements can add majesty to your platform presence.

Hinder?

Certainly. Gestures can get in the way by being:

◆ **inappropriate**

◆ **badly timed**

- ◆ **repetitive**

- ◆ **meaningless**

- ◆ **poorly executed**

- ◆ **contrary to what's being said.**

Let's take a simple example. Consider the word 'big'.
How would you express 'big' normally? Probably by
holding both hands far apart. Now use only one hand.
You had to stop and think, didn't you? Yet it is possible
to signify 'big' with an elegant sweep of one arm,
starting with the right hand in front of the left breast,
palm inwards, and sweeping upwards and outwards, past
the chin and ending with the arm fully extended in line
with the right ear, palm outwards.

Inappropriate

Consider using the two-handed gesture that looks like
you are holding a large parcel, while saying: 'I grew up
on a big farm.'

Now try using the elegant one-armed sweep while
saying: 'The fish that got away was this big.'

Timing

Gestures that illustrate what you are saying should be
started just before you say the words. Point your finger
first, and then say, 'I went that way.' Now try saying the
words first and pointing afterwards. It's like a film in
which the sound is out of sync with everything else, or a
parody by anarchic comedians.

Too many

Gestures can be repetitive. You can also overdo gestures by trying to illustrate everything you say. Once again, it will look like a comedy routine. Try illustrating everything in this sentence:

I would rather be a small fish in a large pond than a big fish in a small pond.

Or this passage:

I felt in my heart that I was among friends.
I felt in my heart my search had come to an end.
I knew in my heart that I'd no longer roam.
I knew in my heart I was finally home.

Doesn't it totally ruin the effect of the sentiment, and look like sign language?

Meaningless gestures are those that are made just for dramatic effect, and are probably better left unmade. One speaker I know developed the unfortunate habit of raising his hand and asking his audience questions like, 'Who would like to make more sales?' Two minutes later it might be, 'How would you like to be able to calculate each person's contribution ... exactly?' Then it was raised with every rhetorical question and every challenge he uttered, to the irritation of his audience, who stopped responding to him.

Some speakers beat time as they speak. The repetitive gestures they use to do this are irrelevant to what they are saying, and do not therefore illustrate the speech. They are just a distraction, no better than a nervous tic.

Poorly executed gestures have similarly negative effects. They could be:

◆ too fast

◆ too small

◆ ugly

◆ across the face

◆ unbalanced

◆ unclear

◆ incomplete

◆ forearm only (with elbows glued to sides).

Poor gestures ruin the overall impression you are making, and make you look unprofessional. That's why you do need to practise in front of a mirror or camcorder. If you are preparing a major speech, once you have mastered the content and words, it is worth spending part of your rehearsal time just observing your gestures and body language.

If you want to leave your audience stirred not shaken, it is vital that you develop and rehearse fluent gestures that add style to your message. I have a number of videotapes of speakers, for example from past speech contests, and I sometimes play them in fast forward. Very instructive. That way I can see how their gestures do or do not work. Most of the women tend to have their upper arms pressed against their bodies, as though held there by Velcro, while their forearms rotate like windmills.

Movement

Should you move around the platform? I think so. I certainly do. However, always move with a purpose, not for the sake of taking a stroll while you ruminate on your topic. Here are some strong reasons for moving:

1. To let everyone in the audience get a better view of you.

2. To check if they are listening – see if their heads follow you.

3. To add energy to what you are saying.

4. To 'place' good points on one side and bad points on the other.

5. To move down an aisle and get among the audience.

Why should everyone get a good view of you? Because those that can't will switch off and create a 'cold spot' in the audience. Cold spots are catching, and can be caused when your listeners:

◆ cannot see you,

◆ cannot hear you,

◆ do not agree with what you have said.

Cold spots are areas of negative energy in the audience which act on others nearby, turning them off as well, or reducing their involvement with the speaker. Cold spots can occur anywhere in the audience, not only in the back row. To minimize the likelihood of cold spots through bad sighting, you should arrive early at the room of your presentation, and sit in every seat that is likely to be blocked. Move the seats, if you can, but be aware of the problem anyway, and move around so that the people in those seats can see you. Then, during your speech or presentation, walk up the aisle or across the audience so that you can connect with everyone.

Watch their heads. If anyone's head doesn't follow you, that person isn't listening, and you need to engage their attention, either by stopping altogether until they look at you quizzically or by raising your voice suddenly.

The late **Ira Hayes** (a celebrated motivational speaker in America) used to throw himself around the stage, often dropping to his knees and throwing his arms skywards like an evangelist. People loved that, although it would be hard to pull it off in Britain. Even so, he projected huge energy and never stood in one place on stage long enough to pay rent! Not for him the protective podium or lectern. He used a stage – the *whole* stage!

A brief word about good and bad points. Remember, *you* know what you intend to say. Your audience will hear it once, at 150 words a minute. You must therefore help them to understand and retain what you say, using gestures and movement as well as words. When you mention 'good' and 'upside' points, go to a particular spot on the platform. For 'bad' or 'downside' points, go to another part of the platform. But be consistent. All positive points in the same place, all negative points in the other place. That will help your listeners to understand more than the words you speak.

Use gestures that tap into the in-built conventions of your listeners. Staying with the 'good' and 'bad' examples: for positive points, have your palms facing upwards, and for negative ones have your palms facing downwards and moving away from you in the manner of 'rejection'.

Here are ten tips about gestures and movement:

1. Do not turn your back on your audience.

2. Do not pass your hands across your face.

3. Make generous, open arm gestures.

4. If you are walking about, stop and anchor your feet when you want to make a telling point.

5. Move with a purpose, just as you might instinctively approach someone when you complain about their behaviour.

6. Avoid pointing your forefinger – it's too aggressive!

7. Remember that certain gestures have different meanings in other countries. Check first. (Avoid the one in which you make a circle with thumb and forefinger. It may mean 'super' to English speakers,

but it means something quite different in certain Mediterranean countries.)

8. Plant your feet. If your toes are forever twinkling, you will lack authority.

9. Stand tall. Touch the ceiling with the top of your head.

10. Smile. It's hard to resist someone who seems pleased to see you. Start the process by thinking of some happy incident that always makes you want to smile. Your face muscles will start to lift, and your spirits will as well. Pick a friendly face and exchange smiles. Others will respond too.

The main message about gestures, movement and body language in general is to speak with power. Power derives from your self-belief, and that in turn derives from the authority that your expertise bestows on you. If you ask yourself a sequence of questions like these, you'll find that even your posture will change for the better:

♦ **What do you know?** (Your subject)

♦ **What can you say about it that is different?** (Your speaking topic)

♦ **Are you the leading authority on your point of view?** (Of course you are!)

♦ **Why do you want to talk about it?** (Your mission or passion)

♦ **Why should anyone listen to you?** (Benefit to them)

I often relate the story of a *Peanuts* cartoon strip. Charlie Brown is walking with slumped shoulders and drooping head. He says something like, 'I'm walking like this because I'm depressed. You've got to walk this way when you're depressed, because if you stand upright you start to feel better ...' It's one of the best lessons I've ever encountered in the relationship between body language and our state of being.

If you want to speak with impact, if you want to stir your audience, and rouse their enthusiasm for your ideas, stand and move with confidence. Let your gestures mirror your self-belief and the power of your ideas.

Radiate energy. Connect with the energy of your audience. Vibrate in harmony with them, and your voice will be like a cathedral organ, stirring, rousing, uplifting your listeners, in a shared experience that will send them out into their own worlds, walking taller and seeing more than ever before. That's the power of a great speech.

In summary . . .

- ◆ Move with a purpose to enhance your meaning.
- ◆ Poor gestures are irritating and get in the way.
- ◆ Move to check that they are listening.
- ◆ Move to give them a better view of you.
- ◆ Follow the 10 tips for gestures and movement.
- ◆ Your posture and comportment will affect your state of mind.